(

MW01120745

THE MINISTRY
OF CONSOLERS

Terence P. Curley

LITURGICAL PRESS
Collegeville, Minnesota

www.litpress.org

Dedication

In loving memory of my older brother

Edmund C. Curley,

"My first editor."

Design by Joachim Rhoades, O.S.B.

1	2	3	4	5	6	7	8

Library of Congress Cataloging-in-Publication Data

Curley, Terence P., 1944–
    The ministry of consolers / Terence P. Curley.
       p. cm. — (Collegeville ministry series)
    Includes bibliographical references.
    ISBN 0-8146-3020-0 (alk. paper)
    1. Church work with the bereaved—Catholic Church.
2. Bereavement—Religious aspects—Catholic Church. 3. Grief—
Religious aspects—Catholic Church. 4. Consolation. I. Title. II. Series.

BX2347.8.B47C88 2004
259'.6—dc22

                                 2004001328

Contents

1. Grief Ministry and Those Who Minister   5

2. Grief Minister as Helper   13

3. Grief Minister as Spiritual Guide   25

4. Grief Minister and the Grieving Child   34

5. Grief Minister and Religious Expression   43

6. Grief Minister and Anniversary Affect   49

7. Grief Minister and Journal Writing   58

8. Grief Minister and Teenage Loss   67

9. Grief Minister and Liturgy Preparation   74

10. Grief Minister as Compassionate Listener   83

Notes   90

Grief Topics and Bibliography   92

Grief Ministry
and Those Who Minister

All ministry requires formation. It must never be taken for granted or done in a cursory way. Ministry is the very life of the Church. In, with, and through Christ, we minister to one another. Our words and actions bear fruit in the way we minister in Christ's name and the name of the Church. We continually ask our loving God to bring to fruition in our ministries the good work begun in baptism.

As Christians we are familiar with St. Paul's emphasis on many ministries. When we consider the Ministry of Consolation once again we turn to Paul and his communal observation: "If one member of the body of Christ which is the Church, suffers, all the members suffer with that member" (1 Cor 12:26). When we explore grief ministry and its many aspects being lived out in community, we really experience what it means to console one another.

Ministry and Community

We are members of the believing community and are responsible for mission and ministry. Our ministry and participation is rooted in the "hope and faith which comes from faith in the Lord Jesus."[1] In imitation of Jesus we need to seek formation for the community to effectively minister. We must recall that Jesus surrounded himself with disciples and sent them forth two by two to bring the Good News of salvation. When we minister in the Ministry of Consolation it is best to keep in mind that what we do is done as a representative of the believing community. A collaborative approach to ministry is essential for the ministry to be lasting. It is also essential for one who ministers to be in collaboration with others not only for support but for ongoing formation.

When grief ministry is collaborative and community based, it can be very rewarding. This may seem like a different kind of remark to make especially about the ministry that intervenes with those who are deeply suffering the loss of a loved one. After three decades of ministering to the bereaved, I am still amazed at the ministry. The encounter with the infinite is immediate and pervasive. As such, these are graced moments in abundance for all involved. When the bereaved receive support and consolation, transformations are almost instantly apparent. This is not always evident in other ministries.

Our rewards are immediate when we witness acceptance and relief by the bereaved as they trust us and relate their story of loss. In every parish there are those who are suffering the loss of a loved one. We need to reach out to them and gently help them realize that eventually their loving God will turn their darkness into light. In this ministry we have an important role to play in the way people go through the process of grieving.

Under the Ministry of Consolation there are a number that focus on particular aspects of grief work. One could minister as a home visitor, liturgical helper, family support, support group facilitator, post funeral follow-up visitor, and more. Some of these consoling ministries require more formation than others. All require ongoing ways to come together with other grief ministers and join in prayer, reflection, and discussion (in accordance with confidences which must be kept).[2] It is necessary for the primary minister not only to identify for the bereaved a support network but also for the minister to choose ways to minister. This requires knowledge about how ministry is practiced.

Finding Your Place in Ministry

The grief minister enters into a covenant for caring with the parish. A covenant means that there is a bond between the parties. There are important considerations as we accept the call to minister. Some of the following may help in discerning how to find your place in this ministry.

1. **Prayer/reflection**

   Prepare through prayer what you believe God is asking. *Are you willing to pray in response to what you feel God is asking you to do?*

2. **Establish relationships inside the bereavement ministry**

   Are you ready and able to find your voice in bereavement ministry?

3. **Personal history issues addressed**

   Have you examined your personal "loss history" and how it will impact on what you do?

4. **Discernment with pastoral staff**

   Are you ready to ask the pastoral staff for approval and support for the ministry?

5. **Formation and support**

   Have you identified how you will be supported and grow in this ministry?

6. **Availability and dedication**

   Are there situations where you would feel it difficult to minister?

Attending to Your Loss History

We bring to our ministry the uniqueness of our own journey through grief. The more familiar we become with our own reactions and responses, the better we can console others. It is essential to keep in mind that our journey through grief colors the way we relate to others. If we have unresolved grief issues, our ministry will reflect it. It is also important not to become a grief minister who is working with the bereaved in order to resolve personal issues from the past. Resolving our loss problems will not happen that way, and it is not a healthy way to confront our own grief. In ministry there is always the important phrase that we have to keep in mind. "Whose needs am I serving?" In the process of discerning we must ask what is best for the other person, the community, and the Church.

Loss Inventory for Grief Ministers

In reflecting on our life's journey it is important that we identify our experiences which we bring to ministry. As you go through the inventory reflect on how your attitudes have or have not changed. Complete the following phrases.

1. I first learned about death and how it happens when . . . .

2. At home we talked about death . . . .

3. My belief in God affected my attitude toward death in the following ways . . . .

4. When I first encountered death I felt . . . .

5. Seeing others grieve makes me feel . . . .

6. As an adult I want to console others because . . . .

7. Some of the difficulties in this ministry I think will be . . . .

8. I believe I can console others in this ministry because . . . .

9. Today for me death means . . . .

Planning Grief Ministry

It is very helpful to carefully plan how grief ministry will occur. Ministerial moments clearly illustrate the many ministries which comprise the total Ministry of Consolation. Members of the believing community are called to certain aspects of this multifaceted ministry. The following will help those who want to minister in their discernment of what their role should be.

1. **At the time of death** (first response ministry)
Who represents the parish at the deceased relative's home? Is there anyone who is prepared to help with basic activities such as phone calls, transportation to airports and railway stations? What about bringing by prepared food? Are you able to be quiet and be there helping with the nuts and bolts of notifications and first issues?

The ritual accompanying this time is called "Gathering Together in the Presence of the Body." Is there a pastoral minister or other member of the parish staff ready to be there at this time? During discernment it is helpful to revisit the ritual itself for gathering together with the family. Here a minister takes a role in nudging toward the spiritual.

2. Arranging the funeral

Is there a parish booklet for the bereaved? Does this booklet explain the liturgy and those who will participate and minister at the time of the funeral journey? Is there a parish staff person or member of the bereavement team who can assist families with options and ideas for the celebration of the funeral? Have they been trained according to the Church's funeral ritual, *The Order of Christian Funerals?* Do you feel comfortable in contacting the family and offering to assist with this?

3. The vigil (formerly called the wake)

This is the first liturgical moment in the death of a Christian. According to the ritual this may be celebrated at the funeral home, the deceased's home, or in the parish church. It should be explained to those who are mourning how the Church celebration differs from the others. This liturgy needs to be carefully planned. Here ministries at the request of the family may take on a variety of roles from helping plan remembrances to offering prayers as the vigil takes place.

4. The funeral and afterwards

The minister as ritual planner has already met with family members for planning the funeral Mass. There are specific options available in the ritual for lectors and family participation. Explaining the purpose and consolation of the signs and symbols surrounding the liturgy is very healing.[3] The consoling grief minister may act as facilitator in arranging for different roles. They may identify for the family how to consider filling positions such as pall bearers, lectors, and offertory presenters.

Ministers who want to help with the gathering after the funeral play an important role as healing ministers of hospitality. They may well help prepare food for the occasion. The parish hall may be offered for the gathering.

5. Spiritual guidance

Parishes are willing to train individuals sensitive to the needs of the bereaved to be mentors. They act as spiritual guides to be there for the bereaved who need to have a one to one relationship. This ties in with the minister as "Compassionate Listener." Follow up visits (two weeks to one month after the death, invitation to support groups.)

6. **Parish support group** *(invitational ministry)*
The "support group" is often called by other names in parishes. These are the more sophisticated groups led by a person with professional credentials. In grief ministry the ideal is for parishes to utilize professionals or trained facilitators from the parish to lead a parish group. The group develops a covenant among its members to participate and help each other in the grieving process. A variety of topics for discussion ranging from the symptoms of grief to coping with holydays, holidays, and anniversaries may be explored. There are many good books and articles on support groups.

7. **Bereavement committee**
The parish bereavement committee works as a sub-committee of the Parish Pastoral Council. It helps to facilitate the entire Ministry of Consolation in the parish. It is a vital committee for initiating and supporting the bereaved in parish events ranging from Anointing of the Sick, special liturgies (November, Advent, and Lent) and with special focus on groups often overlooked such as children and youth.[4]

Professional Referrals

It is important for a support group to be led by a professional since it is dealing with intense mental health issues. When these mental health issues become paramount in response to grief, the grief is characterized by the term "complicated." This means that the bereaved need professional assistance in coping with loss. Parishes are more than capable in assisting people who are suffering from normal symptoms. There has to be a professional referral when it is evident that there is depression or other ways that demonstrate an inability to cope. Good referrals to professionals familiar with treatment for those suffering from complicated grief ought to be made. It is always best if the bereaved person with pastoral support makes the call for professional help.

Conclusion

We cannot attend to the Ministry of Consolation without attending at the same time to ministers. Ministry and ministers define with God's help how consolation will take place for the bereaved.

Ministry Notes

1. All ministry requires ongoing support and formation.

2. There are choices as to how and where to minister in grief ministry.

3. Grief ministers have to be aware of their own experiences of loss.

4. Through praying for guidance and discerning with others we are better ministers.

5. Always inquire as to what the parish/college/hospital, etc., will provide for ongoing formation in grief ministry.

Grief Minister as Helper

We are called to console one another. Unfortunately, mistakes are made when inappropriate remarks or platitudes are offered. We, like our society, can be callous and expect people to let go of their grief quickly.

We need to cultivate ways to prepare ourselves to know how to respond. One of the best things we can do is to reflect on our own experiences of loss and the way we either managed or failed to manage grief. As we do so, we should ask ourselves what comforted us and helped us put our grief into a broader spiritual perspective. When we are reflecting, we should not limit ourselves to these immediate experiences of intense grief. Rather, think about the times after the funeral is over, when life has returned to normal but then suddenly a sound, smell, or situation intensifies the lurking grief bringing it to the fore once more. It is those times when we can insert our losses into a broader spiritual perspective by thinking of our loved one's place in the universe of God's love.

In situations where we want to help, we ought to keep in mind that the bereaved receive comfort from our being with them. Being with them is often enough. Better still is to help them express how they feel and talk out their loss.

Caring for the bereaved may entail everything from house sitting to helping them make funeral arrangements. Instead of feeling paralyzed or empty when we encounter grief, we can experience God's love. Grief experiences are converted to hope when we allow ourselves to journey with the bereaved through darkness. We should try to give the bereaved permission to express feelings and know we are not going to tell them to pull themselves together and don't cry. By letting the emotions out, we help them begin to let go which is the beginning of the grieving process.

We know a lot more today about grief reactions than in the past. Studies in crisis intervention provide us with insights and ways to console ourselves and others. How we actually respond does make a considerable difference in the way people manage loss.

Grief Phases

Mourning the loss of a loved one is characterized by certain phases. It is difficult to assign rigid time limits to the phases as they differ due to our "loss histories." It is better to think of grief as phases rather than steps. The literature of loss has been greatly assisted by steps being put forth for death and dying. Even with those steps we have to realize that it is not necessarily a "step theory," which means that we go from one step to the next. It does not always work that way.

When it comes to bereavement, we have to realize that there is no complete theory for grief. If there were a simple approach with a beginning, middle, and an end, then all we really would need is just one book that would take care of everyone. We realize this is not the case nor will it ever be like that. One size does not fit all.

"Phases" illustrates that there is considerable flexibility regarding time durations and also the intensity of emotions. The phases illustrate general characteristics of grief to keep in mind while ministering to the bereaved.

1. **Initial phase** (time of separation)
The initial phase of numbness and shock is best approached with an open mind. There is also at this time protesting the loss, which may be exhibited through avoidance or denial. It is definitely a time that is disorienting. The disorientation is not illness. Rather it is normal and to be expected in the face of the shock.

Allow the bereaved to grieve. Don't recommend alcohol or other drugs as a solution to grief feelings. If medical intervention is necessary, approach it cautiously with professional help. Alcohol and other drugs just mask very natural responses.

Don't be afraid to cry with the bereaved. Share your faith during this time in non preachy ways. Offer to read the Bible with the bereaved or look over potential readings for the funeral if asked. Offer to pray with the bereaved. Simple prayers are best in these situations. Remember that familiar prayers comfort during confusing times.

Grieving is a process of remembering and letting go. It is difficult to achieve harmony between the two. As the intensity of grief gives way to a calmer period, allow the bereaved to talk and reminisce about the past. When you share with them, you are helping them to redefine their relationship with the deceased. By doing so you are helping them change their perspective. This is one of the most difficult tasks we associate with grief work. It is essential that the bereaved accept and resolve loss by recalling memories and through faith experience the hope that they will be reunited with their loved ones again in the Kingdom.

Awareness of Grief Process

Everything in our culture is done entirely too fast. We shop, eat, work, and even recreate at a very fast pace. Very often grief is treated in the same fashion. People are not allowed to really process their feelings. Too much too soon is expected of them.

In the workplace we find that well meaning co-workers may not know how to relate to the grief stricken. Very often avoidance and denial is practiced. Others feel that in a matter of a few weeks everything is back to "normal," and many believe an even shorter time is all that is necessary for the bereaved to be over the grief. This shows that there is an ignorance in our society about grieving and the process.

We must keep in mind that grief is an intensely personal response. There are some overall characteristics that can help us to generally appreciate what is happening to the bereaved. Grief is cumulative and how we have done in the past greatly affects grief's outcome. If there are many losses and we have had trouble accepting them, then it will certainly be more difficult.

Circumstances vary among losses. If there is a sudden death or death by violence (from suicide or murder), the initial time of shock will be longer and more intense. We can expect someone to be numbed for at least six to eight weeks when there is a loss of someone with whom there was a strong affectional bond.

The severing of a bond is as if part of ourselves has died as well. Many symptoms accompany this initial time. Due to the intensity of what is called "high grief," a person may have some of the very real physical symptoms we associate with loss.

Symptoms Accompanying Loss

It cannot be emphasized enough that these are normal initial symptoms associated with grief. Only when they linger for a length of time beyond the initial phase is there the possibility of more serious concerns. Then professional help ought to be sought.

As a mental health counselor I have counseled and facilitated numerous bereavement groups throughout the years. What I have always noticed is that the bereaved need reassurance that they are not mentally ill due to these symptoms. Everyone can help them by being aware of what is occurring for them while they grieve.

- It is not uncommon to feel a tightness in the throat and heaviness in the chest.
- Sighing.
- An empty feeling in the stomach.
- Loss of appetite or a desire to eat more.
- Feelings of restlessness and looking for activity.
- There may be a desire to smoke, drink, or use drugs (especially tranquilizers).
- Difficulty in concentrating.

- Aimlessly wandering and forgetting to finish household chores.
- Difficulty sleeping.
- Need to tell and retell the story of the loved one's death.
- Mood changes.
- Angry or agitated at the slightest things.
- Anger that is misdirected toward the wrong person.
- Intensely angry at loved one for "being left."
- Crying at unexpected times.
- Sensing the loved one's presence, hearing his or her voice.
- Expecting the loved one to come home any minute.
- Assuming mannerisms or traits of the loved one.
- Yearning to be with the loved one or see him or her again.

These are normal grief reactions as we initially experience the shock of realizing that our loved one has died. This is not an exhaustive list. It is meant to assist us with some overall aspects of initial grief. The grief counselor or minister in being aware of their reactions can expect them and let their impact determine the openness to ministry.

2. **Second phase** (separation and transition)

After approximately two months there is a new realization that the loved one has died. Very often this is the time when the bereaved need the most help. They find themselves alone and aware that the death has occurred. We can help by being aware of this when we communicate with them. It is during this time when those who are mourning may well need a "compassionate listener." This listener will help them to sort out all of their feelings and accept the loss.

During this phase, the numbness which anesthetizes the body wears off. Now certain emotions surface such as anger, feelings of powerlessness, anxiety, guilt, or helplessness. Here again we are talking generally and this general perspective should always be kept in mind.

It is necessary for the bereaved to recall the loved one in many ways. There is the very real transition in their minds about the loved one. They are moving in their thoughts from having someone who was physically present and now is no longer with them. This is no easy task facing all of us as we do "grief work." (Chapter 10: "Grief Minister as Compassionate Listener" details this aspect of ministry.)

3. **Third phase** (separation and reorganization of one's life)
This is the phase whereby we begin to readjust to our loss. Does this mean that grief has ended? The answer is no. There is really no time limit for grief.

After about six months the bereaved usually are better able to cope. They are at a time when they can rejoin activities they did in the past. Once again their lives are becoming balanced.

What to expect (important scenarios relating to the grief-stricken)

Separation	Transition	Reorganization
Minister is there to reassure the bereaved	Minister is there to listen, offer perspective	Anniversaries Prayer Coping-journal writing
Minister listens to losses	Pray/spiritual guidance	

It is best to visualize the "grieving process" according to the above categories. There are many ways to talk about how we grieve. Some theories are more involved than others. This approach takes into account the chaos and it's transition toward that time when our lives begin to reorganize. The following is a scenario of the first six weeks of grief and what people go through early on while they grieve. You can develop this or some other kind of "grieving guide" to assist in the ministry.

WEEK ONE
Shock and numbness—following the shock and numbness comes protest and denial. There are both physical and behavioral changes for the bereaved. We noted the physical. Some of

the behavioral changes are the lack of focus evident in the inability to make decisions, feelings of being broken or shattered. Irritability is often exhibited due to the extreme stress. Look also for signs of being distracted. It is important that with the distractibility caution be taken especially while driving a car or operating machinery. The minister needs to make allowances for their behavior, which can make attempts to minister difficult. Upsetting mannerisms such as sighing or crying can also impact a minister's willingness to "be there" for the people.

WEEK TWO

Even though the funeral has taken place, there are still strong feelings of "unreality." It is still difficult to accept that the death really has happened. The wake and funeral may take on a dream-like quality that someone else experienced. There are financial and legal matters to be taken care of. By now the deceased's will has been read. In families there may be tension due to the last will and testament. Everything from anger to gratitude may be expressed.

WEEK THREE

We must keep in mind when visiting the bereaved that grief is much more of a process that must be gone through than the recollection of an event. It is still very early and the shock and numbness along with behavior has not noticeably changed. The bereaved are still trying to "sort things out." There is the hope to make some sense out of everything.

WEEK FOUR

Initial symptoms still remain. We may hear a yearning and searching by the bereaved for their loved one. At this point photographs or family albums may be opened. The spiritual wondering and need for prayer may surface in better ways now. There may well be the need to have some prayers help match the bereaved's moods. Some ritualizing will take place with the "month's mind Mass."

WEEK FIVE

Feelings of isolation may be continuing from the bereaved. Staying at home alone may be a real burden. There may occur some mild confusion. The bereaved may still inadvertently think the loved one will call on the phone or come in the door any minute. They even pick up the phone to share something only to catch themselves and realize that the loved one has died. This can be very troubling for those attempting to relate to them and move the bereaved along in the process.

WEEK SIX

It may take this long or even longer before the bereaved are ready to seek some help. Help may appear with someone willing to visit and be "Compassionate Listener" or joining a Prayer or Support Group. Now the bereaved may start to become proactive and seek some direction as they journey through grief.

Grief comes in many ways for all of us. Grief like ourselves is unique. As we noted "one size does not fit all." However, there are aspects which we share. Dealing with our emotions as grief ministers is a formidable challenge as we reach out to help those who are mourning. It is a special time of self-discovery for the bereaved and also for ourselves as we minister.

Developing Skills for Ministry

One of the most difficult encounters facing people is how to relate well to the bereaved. People agonize over the right words for the condolence cards or a conversation they may have with the bereaved. This ministry is avoided by many not out of a lack of concern as much as an anxiousness and fear of doing or saying the wrong thing.

The anxiousness experienced by people about bereavement highlights the need for developing skills in communicating. Considerable anxiety may be avoided when we catechize or teach how to go through life events and find meaning. As a Church we have to be careful not to contribute to the denial by avoiding topics that all of us have to deal with in life.

Preparation for ministry training and acquiring healing skills has to be provided. Role playing and appreciating what it means to be with the bereaved can make people be more effective ministers of care to the bereaved.

The following scenario illustrates the need for proper ministry formation and reflection.

Conversing with the Bereaved

> Grief Minister (G.M.): "Hello, Brenda, I just thought I'd give you a call to see how you are doing."
>
> Brenda: "Everything's going along."
>
> G.M.: "Are you getting things done?"
>
> Brenda: "I'm not sure about a lot of things. It's pretty confusing."
>
> G.M.: "It's still very early for you. You must still feel numb."
>
> Brenda: "That's just how I feel. I still cannot believe he died."
>
> G.M: "I'd like to drop by to see you."
>
> Brenda: "That's really kind of you. I think I really need company."

This conversation is a brief way of offering some possible conversations with the bereaved. It requires that the grief minister who wants to be of help be aware of how a conversation could likely take place. It also sharpens ministry listening skills. What did you really hear now that you are better acquainted with initial symptoms? How well did you listen to the bereaved needs? Did you use open-ended statements in order to better engage the bereaved person? These are just a few of the questions and observations for a pastoral ministry seminar. The questions are open-ended and will inspire more remarks and observations for the ministry.

In chapter 10, which is entitled; "Minister as Compassionate Listener," we will explore in detail the importance of developing better listening skills for ministry. Listening and being present to others while they grieve has been called the silent side of communication. It is this ministry of being a healing presence to the bereaved that is most helpful. No one should shy away from this as it is a very rewarding skill that can be acquired.

Is There a Time Limit for Grief?

Many questions face us as we begin grief ministry. The bereaved often ask the question about when will this all be over. It is very important that the bereaved not be misled. There really is no time limit as is evidenced by anniversaries. Anniversaries are a major concern for grief ministers ("Anniversary Affect" is treated in chapter 6).

Anniversaries are the best ways of showing how grief has no time limit. All of us are aware of certain dates and times of the year when we recall our loved ones who have died. The more sensitive we are to this reality, the better we can be caring and empathic toward the grief-stricken. Going through the process we learn that bereavement is something we accept; we may never fully get over it. Rather we learn to cope with loss. This is especially true of those whose loved one's death has caused a change in their life condition. When someone becomes a widow or widower, we don't cease to be one after so much time has elapsed. We have learned to cope with our new status. This new status was especially important in the early Church when there was the order of widows—those who had gone through bereavement and were now able to help others because of their empathy and reintegration into the Christian community.

Needed Resources for Grief Ministry

Losing someone we love is a shattering experience. We need to call upon resources that help the bereaved to rebuild trust and hope. Immediately following the terrible events of September 11, there were many prayer services and words of consolation. A considerable amount of hope continues to be given to the families of victims in those early words and prayers that stay with them in their extended time of bereavement. The prayers and psalms offer the bereaved a context through which they can grieve. As such these initial comforting words become a touchstone to return to in times of stress and loss whether it is a week or ten years after the loss.

In grief ministry the Psalms are a cornerstone for both the bereaved and the compassionate minister's encounters with grief.

The Psalms play a large role in the formation of the grief minister who acts as a "spiritual guide" (Chapter 5 treats Spiritual Expression and chapter 3 "Spiritual Guides").

We have noted the importance of children and teenagers in grief ministry. During the second anniversary of September 11, children were included in the remembrance ceremonies in New York. It was heart rendering to see them read names of victims, including their own fathers, mothers, siblings, grandparents, aunts, uncles, and friends. We could not help but feel the pain of families who suffered such a tragedy.

This emphasis on children focuses both our sympathies on the young who have suffered, but at the same time we are hopeful that these children will cope and grow in their spiritual development just as they develop physically. Seeing the young we are always hopeful of the promise of emerging life (chapter 4 will detail the role of the grief minister and the grieving child).

The ministry of consolation is a multifaceted experience of service in the Church. As a ministry it serves a variety of intense needs facing community members while they struggle with separation and loss in life.

Effective ministry requires that we connect our very selves to what we say and do. Our being present to others is an intensely spiritual reality that must be grounded in appreciating our life's story as we listen to others. There are some dos and don'ts which relate to how we are present to others.

Dos and Don'ts (The Importance of being in the right Framework for Ministry)

Some dos and don'ts can serve as a framework for familiarizing ourselves with better ways to bring healing and hope for the bereaved.

- *Be present as soon as possible when you hear about a death.*

- *Avoid offering platitudes.* Such remarks as "It's all for the best." "It was meant to happen" or even to say at that time "It's God's will." Remarks such as this are untimely for the bereaved. While ultimately we do have to accept

and with God's help we will accept that death has occurred, we need to process that acceptance.

- *Do not simply offer "sympathy." Be empathic.* This means
  placing yourself in the other person's position. Rather
  than say "I am sorry." It is better to say "this must be
  very painful." The latter is more engaging. Use open
  ended questions such as "How do you feel today?"

- *After the funeral realize that the bereaved still need to tell their
  story of loss.* They need to ritualize the loss. This may entail looking at photographs or praying with them at the
  cemetery.

- *Become more familiar with the "grieving process."* Appreciate that it is part of the life cycle. There is a spirituality to
  be cultivated with life's losses.

- *Rituals redefine new relationships with the deceased.*

- *Anniversaries, family celebrations, holidays need to include
  ways of remembering the deceased in the context of the Body of
  Christ.*

- *Don't buy into society's time frames.* You know from your
  own experience how long grief lasts. Don't avoid the
  subject because the loss was a month or two ago or ten
  years ago.

- *Inquire how everything is going.* If you feel close to the person, offer to help with tasks which have to be accomplished. You may offer to help clean or deliver clothes
  etc. to the St. Vincent de Paul Society, Catholic Charities,
  or other suitable charities.

These are a few ways that we can begin to reassess how we
bring care and comfort to those who are suffering losses. In
doing so we also bring images of healing and hope in own lives.
Our ways of relating in purposeful ways bring light to the other-
wise darkness and chaos we call grief.

Grief Minister as Spiritual Guide

Being a grief minister requires ongoing formation. A major concern is the ongoing development of a spiritual outlook toward life. This ministry is very involved with spiritual matters facing both grief ministers and those whom they serve.

Throughout the years I've been ministering to the bereaved I have heard whispers about "grief ministry" as depressing or negative. Some have even ventured to ask me: "How can you do the work you do? It must be very depressing to deal with death?" How far from the truth are such remarks! My response has always been that this ministry is about life not death. It is eternal life and the consolation of believing in the Reign of God.

Questions about this ministry and its meaning continue in our society which is in so much need of evangelization. Proclaiming and living the spirituality of this ministry gives the world a witness to eternal spiritual values. Spiritual guidance and prayer are cornerstones for every ministry. This chapter highlights how spiritual guidance is an essential part of grief ministry. All that we do and say throughout bereavement ministry focuses on how well we provide consolation from the Source of all consolation.

Grief ministry is synonymous with the Ministry of Consolation. It is in the consoling that we find the spiritual guidance from the One who gives us all consolation and hope. Providing spiritual guidance is not so much a learned skill as it is a gift. It involves being with people and involves listening and hearing. It is more often the singer and not the song. It is sharing faith not knowledge. The grief minister brings his/her compassionate vision of life to those whose lives are out of focus or can only try to see through their tears. The grief minister is a guide and companion for those who are trying to sort out what living with loss now means for them.

Giving Guidance

Gerald May in his *Care of Mind, Care of Spirit, A Psychiatrist Explores Spiritual Direction* gives us the following insight about who provides spiritual guidance:

> Spiritual guidance can apply to any situation in which people receive help, assistance, attention, or facilitation in the process of their spiritual formation. This applies not only to deepening one's personal realization of a relationship to God, but also to the dynamic living-out of that realization in the actions of daily life. Spiritual guidance can come through almost any conceivable channel. Certainly it can occur in the church or other religious community settings, but it can also come from friends, family, coworkers, scripture, nature, art, and a multitude of other sources.[5]

Spiritual Needs

Spiritual guidance is necessary when loss occurs. This may be when a family first hears a diagnosis. Guidance is needed by the patient and the family to go through the experience. This guidance may take the form of helping everyone to accept and care for each other as Christians. Individuals and families are thrown off balance when end of life illnesses occur.

During hospice care we find many examples of the need for spiritual guidance. Hospice is a special kind of care for patients and families when a life limiting illness no longer responds to cure-oriented treatments.[6] Hospice acknowledges that life is finite and that at a certain point medical interventions will not restore physical health. Acknowledging this end means that the focus is now on comfort and preparation for both the patient and his/her family. The hospice worker may well be a grief minister who "assists in the transition process to act as spiritual and emotional guides during an individual's final journey."[7]

During the time of serious illness and the death of a loved one, many cries for spiritual guidance may happen. The grief minister often functions as helper, compassionate listener, ritual planner and often a friend during bereavement. A spiritual guide by his or her presence, listening, and words offers guidance. On occasion there will be questions about God, the afterlife, suffering, forgiveness, guilt, and other spiritual topics. Questions or remarks may surface when we least expect. The hope is in preparing for the ministry with other ministers that the grief minister will discuss spiritual situations facing the bereaved and strategize on helpful interventions.

Keep in Mind

The spiritual guide is not there to give answers or rescue the bereaved from their fears and doubts. Effective guides are those who assist the grief stricken in activating their inner resources of faith and trust in order to welcome into their lives more spiritual ways of coping. Guides are there to help the bereaved as companions who show them the way, sometimes not even with words. They are a spiritual presence, reminding the bereaved that they have the spiritual support of the entire community. The grief minister as a representative of the community is sharing with the bereaved the Church's compassionate vision of hope. Carolyn Gratton in her *The Art of Spiritual Guidance* clearly spells out what being a spiritual guide entails:

> The guide is there to help with the interpretation of present crises or transitions, both by stimulating the person's own imagination and empowering him or her to appraise a new vision for the future.[8]

The guide is most helpful when he/she has lived through a time of searching for meaning. When the guide is one who has had to let go of emptiness, anger, searching, guilt, feelings of abandonment and so many other aspects of loss, they become better instruments for contributing to the spiritual well-being of the bereaved.

Pastoral Moments and Guidance

Ministry to the bereaved as with many pastoral moments requires guidance. Spiritual guidance is sought by those who want to know what they need to do for their loved ones and themselves. Let us look at a few of these times keeping in mind that the grief minister is there to interpret crises and give spiritual guidance and direction.

Early moments. These moments occur when we first hear about someone who is seriously ill in the parish. The grief minister as pastoral visitor assists families with spiritual and sacramental matters. When the grief minister is familiar with the sacrament of the sick, he or she can be very helpful. In keeping with the words of the Apostle James, "Is there anyone who is sick among you? Let them call for the elders of the Church," the grief minister can be the one who helps families call for the anointing.

When there is serious illness, families often begin to become paralyzed as to what to do. They are in need of guidance as they anticipate the death of a loved one. Halting, confused conversations about the funeral take place. There is often guilt at thinking about addressing future arrangements. At that time the loved one's journey in life is vivid for the bereaved. They are in need of a personal caring way to live through these difficult moments.

The grief minister is one who listens and offers ways to express love for the loved one at the end of life and in death. When the grief minister has already visited the family before the death occurs, it is much easier to offer spiritual guidance. There is a connection with the family who see this person as someone who was with them in their difficult times.

Throughout the two days of the funeral the Church fills the time with prayers for the deceased Christian. It is the grief minister who gives guidance to families who have not had a funeral in years. Grief at this time can be very chaotic and confusing. When the grief minister is available during the rites, their presence offers spiritual guidance.[9]

Condolence call. Within the first few weeks after a death, a condolence call to the bereaved may be scheduled. At that time the grief minister visits with the grieving parishioner and is supportive. It is still very early for the bereaved in their grieving experience. Certain questions may surface at this time. Some of the questions are painful, such as: "Why did he have to leave me?" "Did I do something wrong for this to happen?" "Will I ever see her again?"

The grief minister is not there to give answers or rescue the bereaved from fears and doubts. Rather, they are to help them move through their grief. It may well be a time when the grief minister will pray with the bereaved not only for the deceased person but also for those left behind. This certainly assists the bereaved in the transition of accepting what has happened and placing it into the wider context of religious faith, hope, and love.

Anniversaries and holidays. Guidance is given by the grief minister as time goes by for the bereaved. There are occasions when a pastoral visit is welcomed by the bereaved. Certain anniversaries such as birthdays, wedding anniversaries, and general holidays are always noted as difficult for the bereaved. They need to live through these times with both spiritual and social guidance. The visit at the time of the yearly anniversary Mass is a pastoral moment that brings healing and hope. Those who are suffering their loss now very silently realize that their faith community has not forgotten their loved one (see chapter 6).

Gift of Ministry to the Bereaved

By virtue of our baptism we are given the spiritual gift to be instruments of healing to others. We are empowered to be with them in their suffering and joy. It cannot be emphasized enough that this is a gift. It is a gift to be given away for our own good and the good of the Church. The grief minister need not be overly concerned about training and learning skills. They can be helpful, but what is most necessary is a willingness to assist the bereaved in developing a more spiritual relationship with God.

Spiritual Transformations

Many changes in outlook occur during bereavement. Grief ministry brings us to a point in our lives where we become more reflective. Ministering to others widens our horizons. As ministers it is important for us to consider the spiritual matters that may concern the bereaved. We are then better able to reflect and prepare for our guiding ministry. Some of the following spiritual matters are prevalent for those who grieve. Each of these is placed in a category for the grieving process. It is good to note whether this matter is brought up *early, mid, or later* in bereavement.

Wanting to cry out to God. (This we often find in early and mid grief.) For some there are strong feelings of being abandoned by God. They need permission to cry out from the depth of their being. They need someone to hear them express their innermost feelings of pain and suffering due to a loved one's death.

Feelings of anger toward God. (This is early to mid grief.) It is not easy for a person of faith to hear someone express anger towards God. We must keep in mind that these are raw emotions trying to find meaning. The grief minister has to remember that the person needs to do this. Always keep in mind that they cannot harm God. Rather expressing hurt is in reality the beginning of a *dialogue* with God.

Deep sense of the ultimacy of life. (This is more reflective and probably occurs in mid and later grief.) The bereaved are aware that life is eternal as they mourn the death of a loved one. This is fueled by a belief system that gives them hope in meeting their loved one again in the Reign of God. This spiritual belief has been called the "heavenly reunion." We hear this spiritual acceptance being voiced in support or grief seminars about a month to two months after the loss.

Better detachment from material things. (This is evident very often during mid to later grief.) The beginning of spirituality is to recognize our dependence upon God. Good spiritual grief work means that there is acceptance of our own powerlessness. Our lives are turned over to God. Spiritual guidance will emphasize our need for *"letting go."* Let's consider what Henri Nouwen has written about our "powerlessness" and learning to trust:

Start simply by admitting that you cannot cure yourself. You have to say yes fully to your powerlessness in order to let God heal you. But it is not really a question of first and then. Your willingness to experience your powerlessness already includes the beginning of surrender to God's action in you . . .[10]

This guidance is in accord with surrendering as the beginning of experiencing spiritual growth. Twelve-step programs for addictions often acknowledge the "spiritual component" of our lives. As such the spiritual is the keystone—acknowledging that we cannot do anything apart from God. Twelve-step programs are spiritual and begin with this as the first step. This step approach has been adapted for ways to spiritually manage our losses.[11]

Search for connectedness. (This noted in mid-late grief.) Searching and yearning is one of the most prevalent spiritual feelings associated with loss. A bond has been broken. Like a shattered vase, the bereaved person wants to find some meaning amidst the emptiness. *"Letting go"* has a "rest of the story." The rest of the story is that we do not let go into a void. Rather in letting go, we reconnect with the Reign of God. In emptying ourselves we find fulfillment. In dying we rise. All of these spiritual aspects amplify spirituality.

Developing a Spiritual Inventory

A spiritual inventory is helpful for the grief minister as he/she ponders the possibilities of the spiritual unrest in others. It makes us more aware of how we deal with grief in our own journey. Often times the spiritual guidance we offer needs to be done according to the gifts given to us in our life's journey. We are pursing what it means to meet the spiritual needs of the bereaved and offer our strength for them. Looking at how we did with some of our concerns and where we received guidance is very helpful. Spiritual inventories shared with other grief ministers during planning sessions can be an invaluable tool for God's grace as we share our journey and best practices with others.

A Spiritual Inventory

While we minister it is a good idea to develop your own inventory. When we write this down, the answers are visible outside ourselves.

1. How do I think about God's will?

2. Do I connect Jesus' suffering with my own?

3. Do I blame God or others for death?

4. Do I consciously or unconsciously blame my loved one for leaving me?

5. Do I feel angry, guilty, or abandoned by everyone?

6. Do I need forgiveness from my deceased loved one?

7. Do I need to forgive my deceased loved one?

8. Have I tried to channel my spiritual feelings of emptiness into prayer or meditation?

9. List three things that you do that you find spiritually comforting.

10. List what you believe are spiritual resources helping you to cope with loss.

Conclusion

In every church ministry it is necessary that we explore descriptions of the ministry. This will make our ministry in the new millennium more effective. Once we begin to reflect and write we can improve and grow. Spiritual guidance by grief ministers is an essential component for consoling others.

Grief Minister
and the Grieving Child

Ministry to grieving children requires preparation and formation. Grief ministers are more challenged in this ministry than many of the other areas of concern with life's separations and losses. Far too often children are overlooked during bereavement. Our goal has to be to include them and gain insights on how we can become more effective in realizing and ministering to children who grieve.

Helping children cope with the loss of a loved one through death is clearly a critical situation. The parish is a setting for healing this grief. Comfort and consolation through religious faith brings the healing reality of God's love to the child.

Children respond in a variety of ways to the death of a loved one. The more familiar grief ministers are with the way children grieve, the better they can help. Very often the child's response to death is startling. We may not expect to see the child "play funeral" or write a letter to Grandpa. The way children think about and imagine death is very important for adult grief ministers to grasp.

Even though a five-year-old generally thinks of death as irreversible, very often she or he thinks that you can outwit it. "If Mommy was faster, she would not have died." The typical five- or six-year-old has confidence in her or his abilities. Death can be overcome. As the child matures we encounter change in their perception of death. The eight-year-old's response might be, "Will we still have a vacation now that Nanna has died?" There is a developmental need for the child to realize how life will change for her or him. They are appropriately egocentric in the face of separation and loss.

The child gives way to the adolescent. Peer group pressure influences remarks. "Only my father died; none of my friends have had this happen." He or she is reluctant to show emotions. After all, the adolescent may have only recently learned to control emotions.

Through the Eyes of a Child

Often adults do not include children in the grieving process. Children have to be involved in the process of expressing their loss just the same as everyone else. We have to keep in mind that unresolved grief from childhood will surface in later years. We must try to perceive grief through the eyes of a child.[12]

In age appropriate ways it is necessary for the grief minister to familiarize him or her self with how children respond to grief. An important dialogue between pastoral care and developmental psychology ought to be taking place. The parish is the appropriate place for speakers and seminars on loss and the coping mechanisms children utilize in the face of loss. Such training will go far with those who seek to assist children experiencing loss.

Special Characteristics

Children go through what is known as "magical thinking."[13] When the child misinterprets or distorts reality, magical thinking takes over. The child may think because they refused to kiss Nana good bye that they are responsible for her death. Children will give us clues about their perception. For our part we need to pay attention. When we realize this our intervention is critical. We need to describe death in concrete ways to children. We live in a death denying culture. Parents and adults have to honestly answer children's questions. We need to learn to be direct and precise in our responses. We can't use euphemisms. They are inappropriate, and the child will only become confused as he/she tries to take what was said literally.

Be Forthright

If we are avoiding painful questions asked in innocence, we have to ask ourselves that basic ministry question. "Whose needs am I serving?" We can easily placate ourselves and our own denial. Our avoidance of what is difficult to communicate to the child only creates problems later on. This means telling them the actual physical causes of the death. "Nana's heart was just too weak to keep beating."

While it may be comforting for us, to say "God loved Nana so much that he took her to heaven," it does not work for children. Children's thinking in concrete terms tend to see God picking people out to take with him. "Maybe this God will take me next since Nana loved me."

Children search for the causes of a death. Language is very important in communicating with a child. To tell a child that their father has "gone away" or that they are "asleep" creates crises. "Why can't I wake them up?" "Did I do something wrong to have them go away?" "Was I so bad that they never want to see me again?"

Redefining Relationships

The earlier a child ritualizes a loss the better he or she does in the grieving process. Letting go really means establishing a new way of connecting. Our responsibility as a Church is to show how new ways of establishing a bond now severed is possible. In order to do this we must be cautious that we do not become part of the problem.

A new relationship may mean especially for the child a new way of imagining God, heaven, and the deceased loved one. Everything is different and the way we relate this is important for emotional and spiritual growth. Imagine the harm that is done when someone makes inappropriate remarks. "You are now the man of the family," "Boys don't cry," or perhaps the most theologically difficult one of all: "God took them."

God's image is not helped when we avoid secondary causes. It is better to explain to the child once again that something went wrong. "The car was in an accident." "The heart stopped beating." "There was too much sickness and her body could no longer handle it."

The image of God who loves and cares for us must always be reinforced. We do not want to attribute the origin of suffering and pain to God. After all, the Christian message is the alleviation of pain. It will be very difficult for the child to relate to God when we even inadvertently make God the cause of pain and suffering. The child will wonder about this type of God. "Is God going to take them next?" The concrete explanation of causes is still the best one for children.

In talking with a child it is important that there be a setting where we can safely communicate about death. Children ought to be encouraged to express how they feel about the death of a grandparent, parent, uncle, or aunt. We also ought not to overlook the death of classmates or certainly a sibling. There is nothing worse than acting as if all losses are the same.

Children and Rituals

Opportunities for ritualizing losses create considerable healing. Rituals are healing vehicles for expressing ourselves and establishing new relationships. Children like adults need to ritualize. Research shows that forming new relationships with the deceased loved ones is very good for children. Our theology certainly gives them many ways to appreciate heaven and the Communion of Saints. We have times in our liturgical calendar (especially November) when parish prayer services can be offered.[14] Children can also ritualize any past losses through simple prayer services. These can range from a remembrance ritual of recalling people who are gone, recalling favorite pets, and even lost objects which could be special toys.

We do not have to wait for a death to examine loss and how Christians come to view it. Grief ministers deal with loss not only when it occurs but at liturgically correct times of the year. A simple lesson about the loss of a pet can go far in helping a child cope with major losses in life.

In the new *Order of Christian Funerals* ministry and participation is emphasized throughout the ritual.[15] The community is encouraged to appreciate the sacred symbols and to express loss from the very beginning at specific moments in the funeral journey. The metaphor of journey is very practical and helpful for parishes. We are all journeying together no matter what our ages. This simple concept, easily grasped by both children and adults is a rich vehicle for teaching about life and death.

Children and Funerals

Among professionals there is overwhelming agreement that children three years and older can go to funerals. This means the vigil and the cemetery as well. It is as one professional puts it the teachable moment. "One should encourage children to express fear, doubt, and curiosity, as well as being open to express one's own feelings[16] concerning death." Another keen insight about children and the funeral is made by Rabbi Earl Grollman. He makes the point that certainly speaks to a child's curiosity and imagination when he tells us that the burial is the best audiovisual aid in the world.[17] A child knows definitively where a person's body is. The question of viewing the body remains best dealt with on a personal basis. If the child expresses much interest in going, they should be allowed to do so for a short time. If the child does not want to go, they should never be forced to do so.

Helping Children with Funerals

Parents have to look for help when it comes to guiding the child with the funeral. If the death greatly affects the parents there is all the more reason to seek out the grief minister. The grief minister is the one who can explain a funeral to children. At the same time by so doing he helps adults. After all adults probably never got this help when they were children.

The grief minister in helping the child often becomes a role model for the grieving child. The minister is the one who helped them through a very difficult time. In the days, weeks, and months ahead this will not be forgotten. For that matter the grief minister truly becomes one who shapes a lasting childhood memory.

Explaining What Happens

Explaining does not mean the pouring out of information. It is really much more than that. The way the grief minister prepares and talks about the funeral communicates deep impressions on the child. The following points will help.

1. What to expect? Unless the child has previously attended a funeral they really are not aware of what happens. The minister needs to explain everything which occurs throughout the time of the funeral. The child will naturally come up with questions. Their questions become the way the minister comes to realize what the child is wondering about.

2. Fill the child in with specific descriptions. Tell them what to expect in the funeral home. Funeral directors are very helpful in allowing children to visit early. They also are aware of how to talk with the child. The grief minister has to remember to give the child very concrete answers. Explain that the body is there and the soul has left the body. The deceased loved one is not asleep—rather his or her soul is with God.

3. You may have to field some unusual questions depending on how old the child may be. They may want to know more about what death is like.

4. Explain that people cry because they miss the deceased loved one. It's all right to cry then and later.

5. Explain that the purpose of the funeral is to pray for the deceased relative to be happy with God. When the child views the body, he or she may want to touch them to say good bye. It is all right for them to do so. It probably is a good idea to reflect as they do so that when people die their bodies are cold and not to be alarmed by that.

I recall being at a family funeral and noticing that my twelve-year-old nephew stayed in the back of the room. His parents were very wise as they told him "You can go up front when you are ready." They didn't overact in any way. Eventually I saw my nephew kneeling down by the casket and making the Sign of the Cross. He really took everything in and knew what to do by observing. This made him far more secure and aware of what he would do.

Grief Ministry and Rituals

Rituals are pastoral care. The grief minister should avoid thinking of them as something separate which takes place before we start ministering.[18] In the *Order of Christian Funerals* we have a resource for expressing loss. The prayers and symbols are comforting for all ages. Explaining the symbols and readings to children is a way of bridging the gap between ritual and pastoral care.

Funerals are not an "adult" experience. They affect all and as such they need to acknowledge everyone including children. While it is not appropriate or practical to make a funeral into a children's liturgy, children can and should have an active role in it. They should be encouraged to present the gifts, including personal drawings or statements about or for the deceased. By including children in the ritual; we not only address their feelings; we also send a powerful message to the rest of the mourners. As we journey some leave us and others join, but we are all traveling together toward the Kingdom. The chain of our families from our distant ancestors before us to our descendants not yet born are together heading for the new and eternal Jerusalem.

A Ministry which Includes

Going through grief is appreciating our belief about life in the Spirit. As with all grief ministry, it's purpose is to bring life and hope and to bring it more abundantly. Without some explanations and prayer services being offered to our young people, we set the stage for further denial and unresolved grief. Such a future ought not to happen. We Christians are suitably equipped to meet the needs of the bereaved in ways far better than our society. Not only does our pastoral theology help contribute meaning, so too does our pastoral psychology.

Through the signs and symbols ritualized in our funeral liturgies, we begin the mourning process in a spiritually enriching and comforting way. We allow young people to participate in ways that stimulate the expression of feelings. Such an expression is cathartic and healing. Our liturgies are meant to release, not control or block our emotions.

Liturgies are not separate from our children. They serve them as well. As we teach our children, we must also care for them no matter what age or condition. In caring we include them in the rich tapestry of the Church's education, life, and ritual for they too are our fellow pilgrims.

In conclusion, the following summations regarding how children and young people experience death in age-appropriate ways is helpful:

Infancy to Early Childhood

Even in infancy there is a sense of loss. Infants certainly do not understand death. However, they experience separation and loss. They learn early on about permanence and separation. This is demonstrated in what may well be their first ritual: "Peek-a-boo."

Pre-school

At around age four there is the realization that something has happened. However, death is seen as only temporary. The child may expect the deceased person to wake up and play with them. Again the usage of correct language about loss with the child is very important.

Elementary School

It is still important that we attribute the right causes for death for the child. It is equally important that the child be included in the funeral rituals. Their participation or exclusion plays an important role in their growth and future grief management. The grief minister must always keep in mind that working with the parent is the way decisions have to be made. The parent has to be encour-aged to talk with their grieving child about going to a funeral.

Adolescence

Death as a social dimension is very real in the teenager's life. The expression of emotions requires considerable patience by adults. We need to learn how to read what the adolescent is really trying to tell us. This is a critical time in which questions about the very purpose of living are being raised in the adolescent's mind.

Grief Minister
and Religious Expression

The crisis of separation and loss cries out for religious expression. Our communication with God is often paralyzed while we endure critical events. Our loss colors everything. How can we pray? Is this an experience that only I really feel? Will this mood ever change?

The grief minister will hear these questions as they converse with the bereaved. The preceding are questions of balance that often occur as we find ourselves totally out of step in our lives. Our prayer life appears to be in shambles. Chaos and confusion controls our very being. Everything about ourselves screams for relief. Where does one turn when bad things happen? Is there an oar to help us steer when we feel ourselves at sea in a fog of loss?

There is the rich resource of the Psalms to help us minister to those who are suffering from the loss of a loved one. The Psalms are a powerful resource for coping with life's tragedies. The grief minister can help the bereaved to realize that by journeying into the Psalms they allow us to explore new ways to express separation and loss. The Psalms can be that oar that helps us steer through our grief. Psalms provide considerable meaning and management for times while we are grieving. They are a powerful resource for guidance.

The Psalms of Lament bring a dimension of meaning for the grief stricken not found anywhere else. Anger, feelings of abandonment, guilt, yearning to be with the loved one, and crying out for meaning are emotions that stimulate us to seek help. Very often the grief minister will note that the bereaved while grieving become confused about expressing feelings in the religious setting. They may find ourselves gravitating toward others and yet still avoiding talking about loss.

Many grieving people do not know how to tell others about conflicts. They lock away their feelings of abandonment and anger. This is common when someone is angry toward God for taking the deceased loved one. Somehow we have been conditioned to misinterpret crying out as a lack of faith. The Psalms are a pastoral way that allows us to express our true feelings.

Rekindling Trust

We can describe the bereaved personality as lacking in confidence or trust. Loss often requires rebuilding lost trust or faith in life as meaningful and a place where there is happiness. Every aspect of life seems to shatter when significant loss occurs. The loss seems to infect our very lives, turning stable faith and hope into new losses. The losses appear to pile up one on another. There is a total disorganization and chaos. For the grief minister relating to the bereaved entails helping piece together broken lives. This requires patience, presence, and empathy in a process which for many goes on for years. There really is no time limit for grieving.

> Mary who is eighty-two years old recently lost her thirty-year-old daughter. The daughter died very suddenly from a heart attack. Mary has always been a very prayerful person. Now, she is withdrawn and tells only a few friends how she really feels. She is angry at God and feels He abandoned her.

The Psalms can be of considerable assistance in comforting Mary. You can see the look of relief come over grieving people when certain Psalms are prayed with them. If we take a few minutes to pray with those whose lives are shattered by loss real healing occurs. The scriptures in the Psalms speak to situations of separation and loss. If we read over the following Psalm allowing our imagination to see ourselves comforting others real converse with God happens.

Psalm 130

Out of the depths I cry to you, O LORD;
   LORD, hear my voice!
Let your ears be attentive
   to my voice in supplication.

The initial crying out of the suppliant illustrates a way to call upon the Lord. The Psalms are truly a school of prayer. They teach us how to talk with God.

If you, O LORD, mark iniquities,
   LORD, who can stand?
But with you is forgiveness,
   that you may be revered.
I trust in the LORD;
   my soul trusts in his word.

The Psalms allow us not to deny what is really happening. Iniquity is part of life and our prayer life has to connect with what is really occurring. Accepting what is happening and still trusting in the Lord is experiencing an authentic faith response.

My soul waits for the LORD
   more than sentinels wait for the dawn.
More than sentinels wait for the dawn,
   let Israel wait for the LORD,
For with the LORD is kindness
   and with him is plenteous redemption;
And he will redeem Israel
   from all their iniquities.

Among all the characteristics of grief, longing is one of the most prevalent. Our souls yearn for fulfillment. We yearn to be with those who have died. This longing is often expressed by searching and even revisiting places which both the bereaved and the deceased frequented in life. The Psalm places our yearning into the context of redemptive trust in the Lord.

There are other Psalms which are appropriate for conversing with God. We are all familiar with Psalm 23. This exceptional psalm sets the tone for coping with loss. So clearly does it express inner feelings that it has become the Psalm for grief and guidance. When we experience loss there is need for guidance "through the dark valley." The metaphor of the Lord as our Shepherd is a helping metaphor especially when we feel aimless and confused.

We turn to the Psalms to process our feelings in a purposeful manner. All of our emotions are chaotic when grief enters our lives.

Anger is a strange emotion in our culture. While its extremes are glorified in movies and television, in reality anger is generated by feelings of hopelessness and loss, and when it is not correctly channeled as an emotion it is very destructive. Consequently for many who associate feelings of anger with the overall cultural denial, it is very difficult to know what is appropriate behavior.

Some highlights from the following Psalm relate to anger. This Psalm not only reveals our real feelings but puts them into a healing context through prayer.

Psalm 22

My God, my God, why have you forsaken me,
    far from my prayer, from the words of my cry?
O my God, I cry out by day, and you answer not;
    by night, and there is no relief for me.
Be not far from me, for I am in distress;
    be near, for I have no one to help me.

As we examine Psalm 22 we are struck by the strong emotion of asking why, yet in the demanding there is also a rekindling of trust. There is a change of mood and a seeking of strength. This is a channeling of the anger by actually conversing with God. The Psalms give us permission to be ourselves in our prayer life. When we pray the Psalms, we do not pretend or camouflage our feelings.

When we help the bereaved to identify with the Psalmist's anger, feelings of loss, and crying out connects us with a deeper spiritual reality. The bereaved are empowered to own their feelings. At the same time these feelings are not thought to be immoral or abnormal. They are an entirely understandable human response to loss. Grief is put into the context of something that has to be gone through with the hope of managing the loss. This means taking the risk of trusting and loving again after one of life's hurts.

Journeying through Grief

Crisis counselors tell us that the sooner we express our losses the better we go through grief. When we delay such expression, we pay a big price. Physical and emotional illness may result when we suppress our emotions.

We are given through the Psalms a wonderful resource in faith. In keeping with revelation, we are given insights about the mystery of life. Through God's self communication we are empowered to cope with our loss as we journey toward the Kingdom. The psalms should be viewed as nourishment and a map for that journey. Reading and eventually praying the Psalms can unlock emotions of grief so we can go forward on our journey.

Prayer of the Church

The Psalms are the expression of faith in the *Order of Christian Funerals* within the section on the *Office for the Dead*. An important option in the new ritual is to celebrate the Office at the time of the vigil. The Prayer of the Church connects us with the entire Body of Christ especially during grief.

"The community's celebration of the hours acknowledges that spiritual bond that links the Church on earth with the Church in heaven, for it is in union with the whole Church that this prayer is offered on behalf of the deceased" (*Order of Christian Funerals*, par. 349).

Coming together as family and community during the intense period of loss can be extremely beneficial. Keeping the hours acknowledges that the whole Church stands with the bereaved as they strain to catch a glimpse of eternity and God's love for us.

In Imitation of Christ

Through praying the Psalms assemblies in faith pray in Jesus voice (*Order of Christian Funerals,* par. #355). Jesus prayed the Psalms during his life on earth. In imitation of Jesus we learn how to empty ourselves to the Father and find real life by so doing. Just as Jesus cried out using the Psalms at his crucifixion so too are we empowered to cry out. When we cry out using the thoughts of the psalmist, we too grow in our hope for eternal life.

Bereavement Exercises and Reflections

1. Recognize the Psalms as a resource for healing.

2. The Psalms help us to express our innermost feeling while grieving.

3. What feelings and thoughts are unlocked for you by the Psalms?

4. How do the Psalms assist us in our journey through grief.

5. Can we accept our loss better by praying the Psalms?

6. In light of your life's journey compose a suitable Psalm.

7. Find a quiet place and meditate on your favorite Psalm.

Grief Minister
and Anniversary Affect

Every parish has to be sensitive to needs facing their congregations. There are times when certain members are very much in need of ministry. The grief minister is a key person for recognizing these critical times for the bereaved. As a grief minister you are also a "crisis minister." As a crisis minister you are sensitive to certain events, occasions, and times that affect those who are suffering from grief. It is necessary that the grief minister possess an awareness of how to address and help meet special needs of the bereaved.

The grief minister is one who must realize that not everyone looks forward to the happiness of holidays. For many, it is a time of great joy but also a season of sorrow. Even those who are not actively grieving are very likely to feel a mixture of emotions. Happiness may be tinted with a sense of loss and sad memories. It is a time of reflection on past holidays and the times of our lives without very important people who have left us. When the tinges of sadness begin to color our anticipation of the holiday the reflective sadness becomes greater. If this happens the grief minister may assess the person as suffering from "anniversary affect."

Anniversary affect touches all of us at one time or another. The longer we live the more losses we have to experience. Holidays and holy days recall happiness since our earliest childhood. Many of these memories cannot be re-enacted. The landscape of memories are peopled by loved ones who have gone.

The looks of joy and surprise when the right present was under the Christmas tree takes place in our bright memories of childhood. The laughter and merriment of that family gathering is impossible to happen again. Brothers, sisters, parents, husbands, wives, and even children have since died. How can we be really happy without them? Is there any sense in celebrating?

Grief Ministry

The grief minister is challenged to be an effective minister during holidays and anniversaries. The minister needs to be prepared to minister to those who with feelings of loss are emotionally more vulnerable than usual. The minister in ministering to others has to be willing to do a self evaluation on how they themselves are doing during holidays.

In ministry it is important to recall that we may experience many intense memories. The minister is not immune to the suffering affecting those to whom he/she is ministering. Some have become friends with families over the years. All the more reason for the grief minister to be aware of having a supportive network for him or herself.

Feelings of loss during anniversaries confirm once again the fact that there really is no time limit to grieving even if the loss is related to a Christmas ten or twenty years ago. We learn to cope with grief—we never get over it or forget. The intensity of a grieving moment or event can dim the nicest of memories. The challenge is to be ever vigilant to put the loss into a context when we experience flashbacks from past losses. A certain song or familiar smell makes us recall the past losses. Many people experience such emotions with deep intensity.

There are continual feelings of sadness for the bereaved during anniversaries. Grief ministers tell us how difficult the holidays are especially for those who are experiencing a recent loss. The first years are certainly the most difficult. There are the constant reminders that life is different. The empty chair, the lack of a presence around the house are most noticeable. The compelling question for the bereaved is: "How can I survive this?" "How can this holiday ever mean anything more for me?"

Normal Anniversary Reactions

The grief minister has to bear in mind that for the most part anniversary reactions are normal. Reactions are telling examples of how the grieving process is progressing from recent losses. Keeping a calendar for ministry to the bereaved is very important in order to keep track of when anniversaries will be occurring. In this way the grief minister may schedule a pastoral visit with the still grieving parishioner at a time of heightened awareness. While it is a different time it can also be a "graced" moment. With a little intervention in the form of a visit it can make a huge difference in a person's life and the ability to move on.

Some of the following aspects of anniversary reactions among the bereaved may be noted:

- *You may note that as the anniversary approaches, the bereaved may confide that there has been an increase in memories, often dreams increase, and other thoughts and feelings surface which they thought were long gone. They may once again think the "lost" loved one is nearby.*

- *The reemergence of symptoms associated with grief may appear. This can be alarming for the bereaved as they may think that they are restarting the grieving process once again. Assurance that they are not going back to square one is very helpful.*

- *Avoidance: this avoidance is a form of denial. The bereaved want to ignore events and memories that may remind them of their grief. They do not want to celebrate holidays. They feel safer if all days are uniform.*

- *The bereaved may not realize that they need to sort out how they will react on the upcoming date or anniversary.*

The grief minister assists the parish by monitoring the impact anniversaries have on the bereaved. The scheduling of parish and family prayer services greatly assists the bereaved in acknowledging their loss. At the same time it assists them in owning their feelings and placing them into a religious context.[19]

Rituals are very important for coping with our emotions during anniversary reactions. They release our feelings and help us to acknowledge that the event is really happening. Rituals may be formal (in church) or informal (at home) and consist of activities that place the loss in the broader Christian context.

The grief minister should always be aware that the bereaved are more than often grieving as a family. During bereavement the family looses its equilibrium or balance. They are in need of adjustments. A family remembrance addresses the family as a system made up of grieving members.

Specific Anniversaries

During the first year after the death of a loved one, certain anniversaries are more significant than others. If we look briefly at some of the major anniversaries and their implications for ministry to the bereaved, we will be better prepared to face the day when it arrives.

Celebrating the "month's mind mass." Approximately a month after the funeral of a loved one there may be scheduled a special Mass. This Mass is for the intention of the loved one's salvation. Families who are still shocked and numbed participate in the liturgy. The participation and ministry offered at this time is healing for families seeking ways to find meaning early on in their bereavement.

Planning the one-year anniversary. This first anniversary of death may be very difficult in the days and weeks before it takes place. The grief minister in keeping in contact with the bereaved may notice that the bereaved are under pressure but not know why. In discussing this first year, some important advice may be given to the bereaved.

1. In talking with the bereaved, the grief minister may suggest that they carefully prepare and plan the day.

2. You may remind them that often families get caught up with their lives and forget that the anniversary is about to happen.

3. Make plans for the day of the anniversary.

4. Keep in mind that the day does not have to be something to be avoided or dreaded. Rather you can manage the grief better by trying to creatively respond rather than reacting.

The first anniversary is a time for the grief minister to make an assessment of how effective the ministry has been with the bereaved. It is more than appropriate to suggest to the bereaved that they do certain things at this time during bereavement. For example, if they are keeping a journal, they may want to do a review. They can look back and see how they have done in order to welcome the future.

The pastoral visit to the bereaved during what could be a most troublesome time makes all the difference. The grief minister is there to reassure and bring comforting ideas of how to go through the day. The role of the grief minister is very evident when someone confides that they are new to the area. If they are trying to work through the loss in an unfamiliar setting, the Church may act as bridge. The bereaved through the familiarity they have with faith may adjust easier through spiritual suggestions. It also is recommended that the bereaved either visit or talk with friends from the area where they used to live.[20]

The eighteen month point. Just when everyone thinks that the grief is over the year and a half point happens. It may seem that everything is back to "normal." Suddenly the bereaved may be surprised by a return of many of the initial feelings of loss. This may lead them to believe that they have really returned to square one. The grief minister is there to explain that this is a legitimate part of the grieving process. During bereavement we are still sorting things out after a year and a half. Once again this demonstrates that there is not a time limit for grief. As another year goes by it will be evident to the bereaved that they are not struggling anywhere near as much as previously.

After two years. It is very difficult for the bereaved to accept that they need to move on. The two-year point often has with it some bittersweet realizations. The bereaved feel better and recognize the challenge that they have to go on with their lives. At the same time there are "misplaced" feelings of being disloyal to the loved one who has died. This is clearly present when a widow or widower has met someone who means a lot to them.[21]

The two-year point as an anniversary or marker point in the bereavement process brings with it many mixed feelings which need to be sorted out. The bereaved need to be assured that there is someone willing to listen to them. This can be very helpful for them and their family no matter what the new circumstances are.

Grief Considerations

Grief ministers play a very significant part in the life of any community. They work with psychological insights and help the bereaved to move beyond those areas of concern. They engage the bereaved in ways to ritualize and accept loss in their lives. They're catalysts for change and healing.

The grief minister should be familiar with the symptoms associated with intense grief reactions—especially on anniversaries within bereavement. The feelings of exhaustion, anxiety, inability to sleep well, loss of appetite, and even a return to shock and numbness are among the symptoms the minister now helps the bereaved to cope with. The grief minister explains that this is not a return to the beginning but a transitory symptom of "anniversary affect."

In many ways the only person really noting how someone is doing after two years may well be the grief minister. Everyone else is either too busy or preoccupied with other concerns in their lives. The grief minister is the one who is there for the bereaved to assure them that they will go through this time-limited period. They can explain "anniversary reactions."

Going Through Grief During Anniversaries

Very often anniversaries tell us about ourselves. We experience some self-discovery as we re-explore the meaning of our relationship with our loved one who has died. They have lived their journey and we are still journeying. What we may discover is how well or poorly we did with our loved one at the end of their lives.

The bereaved may find themselves during anniversaries with a need to verbalize feelings of emptiness and loss due to their thoughts about how they may have inadequately responded to the needs of a dying loved one. They may well be seeking forgiveness for not being there. These regrets and guilt can be overwhelming and may impede the grieving process.

There are also those who due to their deep attachments cannot "let go" of the relationship. Not letting go is about them and not necessarily about grief. They may be very controlling in every aspect of life. Death takes them by surprise as they did not allow for such an eventuality. The grief minister has to stress a spirituality of "letting go" and trusting in God. It may be obvious to the grief minister that the level of faith maturity of a bereaved person may be lacking by not accepting the will of God. After a length of time the acceptance of the event and God's will is necessary for good grief.

Conversations with the bereaved may open up all of the emotions we associate with grief. The grief minister who enters into the bereavement of others has to be prepared for such realities. It is the grief minister who often stands alone in the community as the one willing to be with the bereaved.

The grief minister is called upon to utilize listening skills with the bereaved during anniversaries. This important skill is often overlooked or forgotten by those who merely "check in" and see how the bereaved are doing. It is important that the minister give the bereaved sufficient time during a visit to recollect or tell their loss story. Be open to sitting and visiting over tea or coffee. Allow the bereaved this "ritual" to prepare to talk with you. The ritual may be having tea or coffee or saying a short prayer. Grief ministers need to enter into the bereaved's world and allow them the opportunity to talk about the loss whether it has been six months or six years.

Grief Ministers and Encouragement

It is the grief minister who encourages those who are grieving to participate in special anniversary activities. This contributes to shaping grief in ways which are healing and allow for better ways to cope. At the same time participation means preparing one's self ahead of time regarding how and to what degree participation is possible.

As Christians the participation ought to include some way of making the day spiritual. A spiritual celebration activates rich resources in faith. Our ability to trust and love again are highlighted through liturgical celebrations. These celebrations help us to remember our loved ones and offer love through worshiping in hope for the Kingdom of God.

A faith filled practice is the memorial eucharistic celebration. To see a family come together and remember a loved one on certain anniversaries puts everything into perspective. The family begins what may be one of the most difficult days of the year with the rich resource of liturgy. At the same time it illustrates a family's faith response.

After the memorial liturgy families gather for breakfast. Some families plan a special event that helps them to stay together for the day. This may be visiting a museum, some historic place, or having a family meal. It may mean going to some place that always has been significant in the family's tradition.

With the help of a grief minister the bereaved can plan ahead and find some real peace. The grief minister acts as an instrument of healing. The bereaved benefit from their presence at the often critical and overlooked time of anniversaries. Ministry at this time is an essential expression of care for the bereaved.

Conclusion

Ministry means being with people. This is especially true for grief ministry when people are in crisis. Serving the bereaved during critical moments such as anniversaries has lasting effects. The grief minister is acting as a compassionate companion to those who are in need of the community's supportive presence.

Grief Minister
and Journal Writing

When I was in graduate school a major professor used to describe himself in ministry as a "player coach." It is amazing after all these years what remarks and insights stay with you. As erudite as he was, the professor knew how to describe what it meant to be with people in their lives. His words aptly describe the way the grief minister enters into the life of the bereaved when he or she helps them with the healing task of keeping a journal. It is a privilege to participate and offer coaching to those who want to give some meaning to their loss through journal writing.

Everyone's journey through grief is unique. How well or for that matter how poorly we progress depends on our ability to do creative grief tasks. Our personal responses are colored by many factors. Among the factors are the bond we had with our loved one, our history of past losses, the circumstances surrounding the loss, as well as other issues such as health, age, and circumstances.

Creative journaling is one task for grief work that also serves as a tool for healing our many hurts. We literally step outside of ourselves as we write our way through some very difficult days. When the grief minister suggests that journal writing is a positive way to go through difficult days significant healing may occur.

Tasks for Grief Work

The grief minister does a real service for the bereaved when they advise them about what grief can do. They can communicate to the bereaved that they allow it to happen, that grief can control and overwhelm their lives. It is far better to manage losses rather than have our losses so color our lives that grief becomes our manager. Managing our losses entails doing important tasks that help us to accept and define what has occurred in our life.

Grief tasks include the necessity of rituals. We need to express ourselves through signs and symbols. Ritual gestures and actions connect us with our loss while allowing us to manage it in healing ways. Through our rituals we put our loss in context and redefine it making it manageable for us in the most difficult times.

Journal writing includes all the elements of a ritual for our necessary response to loss. As we write about ourselves and our thoughts and feelings, we utilize symbols and gestures to do so. We turn the act of writing and reflecting into a ritual. Making the commitment to "journal" during this difficult time imposes parameters on our grief. The commitment—daily reflecting and writing is repetitive which imposes a ritualistic structure on us especially if we set aside a certain time to do so. The best journal writers usually have a set time and place to reflect and write each day. Having this structure imposes order amidst the turmoil and confusion of initial grief.

As we write we reflect on the loss and are able to step back from the most intense feelings, making them manageable within the confines of the text we're writing. Writing about our losses helps us to let go of those barriers and the chains that bind us to our loss.

Spiritual Tasks

The presence of the grief minister is a reminder to the bereaved that there is the spiritual dimension of grief. The grief minister reminds them that along with the physical and emotional expressions accompanying loss is the simultaneous need for spiritual expression. Journal writing is a way to express our innermost feelings. It is a suitable way to help ourselves and very often to honor the memory of our loved one who has died.

During times of loss the spiritual task that confronts us is letting go of the physical relationship and welcoming a new way of spiritually relating. This all important task literally tests our faith. While we grieve our faith and belief may well be troubled. As we journey through grief our journaling can be a valuable tool for healing our brokenness both in the present and future.

Resources in Faith

The grief minister can help the bereaved with the good idea that before we begin writing our journal we do some "scriptural home work." The Scriptures are filled with images and healing ways to manage our losses.

When we meditate on certain Psalms we receive healing interventions from our loving God who shows us ways to arrange our thoughts for effective healing through journal writing. We need ways to organize the chaos which surrounds us while we grieve. Our very thoughts about what is occurring needs some structuring. The Psalms help us to sort out what is happening and provides ways to express and manage our loss.

In this ministry to the bereaved, we can easily see ourselves opening up a Bible with the bereaved. Together we can review certain psalms that speak to the grieving process and serve as entry headings for our grief journals. Often the grief stricken will choose a Psalm quote as an entry and catalyst for thoughts to write about.

Feelings of loss. We have feelings of abandonment, guilt, emptiness, anger, and yearning to be with our loved one. We are gifted with Psalms which bring healing and are a catalyst as we fashion our grief journals.[22] Initially Psalm 130 speaks to our loss.

> Out of the depths I cry to you, O LORD;
>   LORD, hear my voice!
> Let your ears be attentive
>   to my voice in supplication.
>   (Ps 130:1-2)

Searching for guidance. Writing a journal in the context of faith requires our surrendering to the Lord for guidance. Psalm 23 provides us with the healing image of the Lord as our Shepherd.

> The LORD is my shepherd; I shall not want.
>> In verdant pastures he gives me repose;
> Besides restful waters he leads me;
>> he refreshes my soul.
>>>>>> (Ps 23:1-2)

Feelings of loss and abandonment. The Psalm writer is very aware of what constitutes loss. Reading Psalm 22:1-6 speaks to our feelings of isolation and abandonment.

> My God, my God, why have you forsaken me,
>> far from my prayer, from the words of my cry?
> O my God, I cry out by day, and you answer not;
>> by night, and there is no relief for me.
> Yet you are enthroned in the holy place,
>> O glory of Israel!
> In you our fathers trusted;
>> they trusted, and you delivered them.
> To you they cried, and they escaped;
>> in you they trusted, and they were
>>> not put to shame.
>>>>>> (Ps 22:1-6)

When grief is yearning and missing. Our lives are so very different we yearn for previous experiences of being with our loved ones. Psalm 42:1-5 helps us to place these emotions into the context of faith.

> As the hind longs for the running waters,
>> so my soul longs for you, O God.
> Athirst is my soul for God, the living God.
>> When shall I go and behold the face of God?
> My tears are my food day and night,
>> as they say to me day after day,
>> "Where is your God?"
> Those times I recall,
>> now that I pour out my soul within me.
>>>>>> (Ps 42:1-5)

Free me of these feelings. We live and wonder about our experience of loss. There is no time limit for grief. Our grief changes as our lives continue. Yet we still persist in crying out "How long, O LORD?" Psalm 13:1-4 verbalizes our human cries about the duration of loss. This Psalm is again another catalyst for thought as we live and write about our losses.

> How long, O LORD? Will you utterly forget me?
>   How long will you hide your face from me?
> How long shall I harbor sorrow in my soul,
>   grief in my heart day after day?
> How long will my enemy triumph over me?
> Look, answer me, O LORD, my God!
>
> (Ps 13:1-4)

Stress Reduction

As grief ministers we can reassure the bereaved that journal writing does not have to be a literary masterpiece. In fact it really does not even have to follow literary rules. What is most important is to keep in mind why we are writing. It is not for publication. Rather, it is meant to bring healing and restore our sense of balance during a critical time in our life.

It is good to emphasize with the bereaved that while we grieve we need to tell and retell our story of loss. This is of great assistance in another primary task for grief; the *acceptance* of the loss. We begin to become more reality based in accepting that our loved one has really died. While we put our thoughts and feelings down on paper or visualize them on a computer screen stress is reduced.

Studies have shown that there is stress reduction when we write about what has happened to us and how we relate to our emotions. In addressing what stresses us we reduce that stress.

Our emotional well-being is enhanced by simply writing in our journal for a brief time each day. The time spent does not have to be lengthy. It may be as short as ten to twenty minutes or even less per day. Our actual time writing may be preceded by briefly exploring God's word. As previously noted making the Psalms our own is good grief work as well as good prayer.

Structuring Our Grief

In grief ministry it is good to acknowledge for the bereaved that during bereavement we enter a chaotic period. Our physical, emotional, and spiritual health is often in turmoil. We need relief and often cry out for ways to give some form or structure to our lives.

Journal writing structures these painful emotions. We step outside of ourselves and express those painful thoughts and feelings in written form. Through describing our innermost stressful emotions, we feel relief from those stresses.

Self-Discovery

Grief radically changes our world view. Our loss experience is so intense we often feel as if time has frozen. How can life continue when everything has stopped? Memories, dreams, and reflections about our loved one are more vivid than ever. The past and frozen present rules our lives.

You may want to relate to the bereaved how the spiritual writer Henri Nouwen found writing about his mother's death as an expression and vehicle for his grief. Shortly after his mother's death he wrote to his father *A Letter of Consolation*.[23] He wrote the letter for himself as well as his father. He states in the introduction about how he needed to "listen to my own inner cries."[24] The value of writing about grief is again stated when he wrote: "Once I started to write I realized how much I felt, how much I wanted to say, and how much had remained hidden during the six months since mother had died."[25]

The psychology of loss tells us that in death our loved ones are more present in our minds than even while alive. The symptoms surrounding grief and how well or poorly we do gives us insight about ourselves. We experience significant aspects of our personality. Everything is brought out in raw relief. This can lead us to self-discovery. We are changing, and through our "journaling" we can write about who we are really becoming in our bereavement.

Better Connections

Often what can accompany our feelings of loss is *disconnection.* In death we sever a physical tie or bond of affection. It is necessary to respond to our gnawing feelings of isolation and even abandonment. To remain "disconnected" puts our emotional stability at risk and slows our progress toward healing.

Journal writing is like dieting. There are many compelling reasons to do both. Like dieting we journal when we are ready, but also like dieting we are urged to begin when there is a need and not wait for the problem to overwhelm us and become the driving force in our lives.

The Grief Experience

While we grieve it is very helpful to become familiar with common symptoms. We may or may not experience all of these symptoms. Becoming aware helps our writing. The flow of ideas and the writing need to be fueled. Our personal story needs to be stated and restated many times over.[26]

Getting Started

Once the grief minister has examined some compelling reasons for journal writing they can in a practical way help the bereaved to get started. They can assure them that the actual nuts and bolts of putting together a journal is not all that difficult.

1. First: *select for yourself the right notebook.* This selection may range from a three ring binder to a computer journal formatted according to your likes.

2. *You may want to include art or poetry or photos of the loved one. Art expresses ways to dialog about loss.* Certain music, art, and poetry capture special remembrances about our loved one. Photos of loved ones can be a catalyst to recalling memories of shared times that are now put into a new context.

3. *Write at a time that is best for you.* It is helpful to select a time of day when you can give fifteen or twenty minutes without interruptions. Don't worry about the length of the entry.

4. *Let your writing flow.* When we let our thoughts be open according to our stream of consciousness, we are by far in a more conducive state of mind for healing revelations. Spiritual unveiling occurs and helps us to experience healing images in our mind. This leads to imaginative writing. Imagination and healing go hand in hand.

5. *Write about fulfilled and unfulfilled dreams and hopes.* When we write about a loved one who has died, many thoughts come to mind. Our loss may well be the death of a dream connected to a loved one's life. Our work with them, partnership in life's ventures, and other dreams fulfilled or vanquished.

6. *Remember in grief you are sorting things out.* While we grieve we have to decide what memories and dreams we will hold onto and what we will let go of. Writing helps us sort everything out.

7. *Focus on how grief is a time for self-discovery.* All of us go through changes and transformations as we go through life's passages. Documenting our changes helps us see ourselves in the present and helps chart our future course.

These are a few suggestions to help get you started on what may be one of the most important journeys of your life. Journal writing is a healing tool that will bring tears and joy. You may want to conclude your time with the bereaved with a suggestion that they begin their writing with a short prayer. An even better way is to pray a prayer with them for journal writing.

A Journal Writing Prayer

O Lord I ask you to direct my writing as I
Write about my grief. Help me to realize that
You will inspire me with healing and hope as
I recall so very much. In your kindness I ask you
Open up new ways of remembering my loved one
(Mention Name) and give me the strength to continue
My life's journey. Amen.

Grief Minister and Teenage Loss

Experiences of separation and loss occur at any time in our lives. We realize that grief is an intensely personal experience. There are characteristics that we share in common. For the grief minister it is very important not to overlook where we are in age and maturity.[27] It does matter where we are in our lives. Characteristics of grief for an older person are noticeably different than those of a child. Similarly the experience of loss for a teenager while sharing in common symptoms is noticeably different. Unfortunately far too often the teenager is the person excluded in our society.

Recent notice has been given to teenagers because of depression. The unhealthy acting out of teenage depression has alarmed us with harm in the form of suicide taking place among this young segment of our society. Our society needs to be more aware of teenage grief and the very definite needs facing them as they confront loss.

Ministers who console have to address the many needs facing the bereaved teenager. The Gospel has to speak to the point of their needs. It is through the word taking form in pastoral care seminars, counseling, and creating an atmosphere of concern that the teenager is able to place his or her loss into the context of faith.

It is no easy task for the grief minister to relate to a bereaved teenager. Their needs are very complex and they do not always verbalize what is bothering them. The following pastoral example illustrates how loss of a sibling affected a teenager.

Mary Ellen came by to talk about her depression over the loss of her brother four years ago. As we talked she noted that she had just celebrated her birthday. She was now a year older than her brother when he died. She had outlived him now even in terms of birthdays. This meant she had to work on developing an entirely new image and relationship with him in death.

Different Aspects of Teenage Grief

The grief minister has to be aware that teenage grief shares common characteristics with other age groups. What makes it different are factors concerned with psychological and physical growth. As with anyone, the teenager is a product of what is happening to them physically and emotionally. The teenage years are in themselves a time of transition. It is not by accident that many cultures have rites of passage for this age group. Somehow what has to be demonstrated is that they are now moving into adulthood. It is a time of intense stress as the teenager wonders not only about physical developments but emotional ones of separating from the security of childhood. They have to assert that they are independent, even though they may have very real misgivings. To complicate matters they have peers who also assert pressure. Culturally there are many expectations heaped upon the teenager.

When I first was studying psychology, I recall a professor giving a very good definition of adolescence. He said that "adolescence is like taking a house with all the furniture in it and moving it across the street." Over the years I've seen this definition ring true for teenagers. It is really a chaotic time. We have to expect everything to be moved around in the transition.

Grief is a chaotic time and sorting everything out is no easy task. When grief strikes the teenager, we have to make certain accommodations. The more we are aware of what is occurring with the teenager, the better we are able to be supportive.

Charting Teenage Loss

In grief ministry there is the awareness that the better prepared we are for loss then the better we will cope. This in no way minimizes the intensity of the moment of loss despite how much we anticipate it. The anticipated loss suddenly becomes very real and final. Being prepared does however help since we've already anticipated the patterns of our response to loss.

Sudden death, however, is very much in a category all it's own. We note this especially when a teenager dies in an automobile accident. It is so unexpected by teenagers who grieve the loss of a friend that the shock is very intense. Most aware communities respond with opening up schools and having crisis counselors talk with bereaved students. Teens being very peer related do well in this setting where they can get help while being with other bereaved teens.

Teenagers feel the pressure of prolonged illness. Whether it is a sibling or a parent such illness affects them deeply. At the same time there is not always the demonstration of emotion. We have to be aware that they are still trying to assume an image of adulthood. Consequently it seems to take longer to see them grieve. Without a societal norm for grief or clear expectations in a death denying culture, teens seem to flounder more than the rest of us. In the face of such confusion, they opt for control of emotions, denial, and an apparent non-caring attitude amidst very real suffering.

The grief minister wanting to chart grief can utilize the "phases" of grief as they apply to teenagers. This will greatly assist the grief minister in anticipating the losses as the teenager goes through the grieving process. If we look briefly at the initial phase, transitional phase, and the time of resuming one's life our efforts to assist young people will be enhanced.

Early or Initial Phase

The grief minister will note that initially the experience is one of shock, numbness, disbelief, or denial. These are some of the prevalent emotions. There is also anger that may surface during this early phase of grief. "How could God take away my father when I was so young?" "Why did God pick me rather than some of my friends who don't even love their parents?" Many questions arise and many are of a religious nature. The feelings of abandonment are very pronounced. The teenager truly feels lost. Life is devoid of meaning. There is this tremendous vacuum that no one seems to know what they are feeling.

Guilt is especially prevalent when there has been a lengthy illness. The teenager may feel selfish because he or she did not spend more time with the dying loved one. They may feel guilty because they did not acknowledge that the dying was occurring. All the defenses and denials are now right in front of them and need to be addressed.

When we lose a loved one, part of ourselves dies. Teenagers feel this as well. In the teenager's world he or she must soon return to school. There they can become very self-conscious. It is very difficult to be the focal point of classmates due to grief. Hidden fears such as how will I now be seen by my classmates and friends surface. Inappropriate questions and remarks can trigger a real emptiness in the teenager's life. The grief minister and other professionals have to be aware of what the teenager is going through. If ever there is a need for a compassionate listener, it is for the teenager experiencing grief.[28] It is a unique challenge to not only be there during this critical time but also to know what the teen is experiencing and is not always able to communicate.

Ordinarily this initial phase lasts for about six to eight weeks. With the teenager amidst all their added complexities, the time span can be noticeably longer. Adults must be patient and understanding of how stressful grief is for a teenager. This is sometimes difficult to understand when there are few outward signs.

Teenagers, especially younger teens, are individual mixes of child and adult. As teens transition through childhood's end they do so at their own pace and schedule. Add to such a confusing state the feelings of loss, and it is very difficult to know how a teen will react. Unless one takes the time to allow the teen to reveal their feelings at their own pace, it can be difficult to assist them through grief. A teen being that combination of child and adult experiences grief in both hemispheres; as a child there may be "magical thinking" still involved in their mind. It might be something they did or did not do; as an adult the teen can rationalize that it is not the case yet the feelings of guilt and depression linger.

The maturity level will determine how grief is experienced and which aspect of the child/adult will dominate. For the consoling adult it is important that we give the teen permission to be who they are: a child, an adult, or a combination who may be confused, hurt, or depressed. The good grief minister will not denigrate or characterize feelings as childish—they are feelings that are always legitimate.

Transitional Phase

Most of us find after the numbing is worn off we have to accept and go through our grief. This is for many the most difficult part of the process. The body has almost anesthetized itself during the initial phase. Now, we realize without the numbing that grief is very painful. For the teenager the question is: "Who can I share these feelings with?" Mistakenly our society thinks that after a few months we return to "normal." This view only serves to have teenagers suffer on their own and perhaps act out inappropriately. During the months necessary to accept and do the essential grief work of sorting out emotions there is a need more than ever for someone to be there. The more present we are without prying into the teenager's life, the more we actually help.

It is usually during the transitional phase when help is sought. The teenager realizes that the pain has to be addressed. We must look for ways to be comforting without taking away their grief. The last thing a teenager needs is to be rescued. Rescuing often consists of not giving the teenager the necessary space to express how they really feel. The teenager needs to be allowed to own his or her feelings.

Support groups for teenagers are more complex. It is not a good idea to have a support group facilitated by another teen. Somehow with bereavement support groups of peers, peer pressure could actually have everyone agree upon life to be seen as truly "empty" or "the pits." It is good facilitation when a grief minister assists the teens in admitting to the chaos and begin to try to sort things out.

Religious faith is an all important aspect of anyone's grief. For the teenager there is also the need to form a new relationship in faith with the deceased. Our gatherings with youth should not avoid praying for those who have died. Not including the losses, even early ones, on our journey only contributes to the denial. Our youth groups, Catholic schools, and parishes need to include grief as part of the journey.

Platitudes do not help the teenager to go through grief. It takes time to process the loss. To superimpose religious statements only generate resentment. Acceptance takes considerable time. Eventually the teenager will come to accept the loss and try to see it as part of God's plan. To say too soon that it is God's will only complicates matters.

Reorganization

The third phase of grief is that of reorganization. This means that the teenager is functioning fairly well and is once again at home with his or her feelings in society. This does not mean that the grief is over. Once again we assert that there is no time limit for grief. We adjust but we are not the same. It is important especially during holidays and anniversaries that the teenager be made aware of the ongoing nature of grief. It never completely ends but we learn to cope.

It takes a lifetime to sort out grief. Teenagers start earlier, and it is a long journey ahead of them. How well they do depends upon the support network and the degree of empathy we are willing to give. In our society teenagers are often excluded since we perceive them as young. Excluding them is a real mistake especially when it comes to grief.

The grief minister's challenge in the ministry of consoling is to include all who are grieving losses. The better the grief minister can make our congregation, schools, and society aware of loss in all of the life span, the better we become at reaching and healing others.

Context of Faith

When we grieve we go through many changes. The consoling minister is there to help facilitate healthy change and more.

Transformation is a key word for grief ministry. What has happened can spark religious faith. We need to help the teenager place his or her loss into the context of faith. They need spiritual guidance as they journey through grief. The moments of loss, the searching and yearning for the loved one, the feelings of abandonment can be placed into the context of faith. For the grieving teenager this is truly transformative when this happens.

We are called to be instruments of healing for teenagers. We must help them face bereavement not alone but with the support of the believing community. Time spent with them is time which assists them with acceptance and a more spiritual life.

Bereavement Exercises and Reflections

1. Discuss the meaning of loss with a teenager.

2. Explore the spiritual dimensions of loss with a teenager.

3. Inquire about how well a young person is doing in managing loss.

4. As consoling ministers, discuss what vehicles or places for healing exist for young people in your community.

Grief Minister
and Liturgy Preparation

Liturgy preparation is an aspect we do not want to over-look when we consider grief ministry. Preparing for the funeral of a loved one is an essential concern for the grief minister. The grief minister is the one who meets with bereaved family members to plan the funeral liturgy. This is a critical moment which often sets the tone for the bereaved going through the grieving process.

Families are in need of this ministry in order to worship meaningfully at the funeral Mass. The grief minister has to keep in mind that the funeral is the introduction to mourning. It is a significant moment for ministry which colors the expression of grief in the context of faith. The consoling minister is a key person in assisting the bereaved at this time of great need.

Paul Irion in his work on funerals and bereavement gives us the following valuable insight as to the importance of ministry at this time.

> The funeral itself is only one part, sometimes even a small part, in the whole psychological process of meeting bereavement. Yet, because of its public nature it is extremely important. It represents the response of the community or the church to the emotional experience of the mourners. Thus, it cannot be regarded as either irrelevant or contradictory to the psychological process of acceptance, release, expression and assimilation that enable the mourner to endure and overcome the tremendous disorganization of his life which has taken place.[29]

Grief Minister's Role

It cannot be emphasized enough how important the grief minister is in meeting with families. Liturgy preparation is far more than just the assigning of roles. While choosing the lectors and gift bearers is important for the liturgy, it cannot be the principal concern. More important is the family's acceptance of the need for a funeral and placing their loss into the faith context.

The celebration of the funeral has many purposes. Among the purposes for a funeral are the following: (1) the ritual and prayers are for the deceased and a sign of our respect and hope for salvation for both the deceased and ourselves. (2) Prayers are also offered for those who mourn. They find comfort through placing their loss into the context of faith and trust in God. (3) The funeral symbols and ritual actions connect us with the eternal and remind us that we are witnessing the completion of the deceased's journey in this world. We are helping them to cross over the waters of death into the Reign of God.

The grief minister has to be aware that in our society we are accustomed to thinking of the bereaved as those being cared for by others during the funeral. Some would even assign a victim mentality to the bereaved. In this way of thinking the idea is do everything for them. They should not be asked to decide anything. This is not really an accurate picture. Even though the bereaved are facing many thoughts and feelings, they too are being called to minister and participate.

Families and friends must minister to one another. The grief minister may act as a catalyst for ministry within the bereaved family. As a consoling minister there is the need to remind the family to think in terms of family and cherish one another. The minister may remind the families about those who are forgotten while they grieve. This is especially evident when families do not include children. Among the elderly very often the aged deceased's siblings are overlooked in their grief.

Ministry and participation in the funeral are not a passive endeavor. Rather, real love and compassion expresses itself within families when they bring healing and hope to each other and the entire family unit.

The grief minister in meeting with the bereaved alleviates considerable anxiety. It may have been years since the family had a funeral. They do not know what to expect. Another scenario is that the family is not all that religious. This is a moment to be present and understanding, helping them to be familiar with the importance of worship. The words given in helping them, in God's grace, will go far beyond the time of the funeral. Again the consoling grief minister is a person of faith who is empathic and caring.

Ritual Awareness

Grief ministers prepare themselves for meeting with bereaved families for liturgical preparation by becoming familiar with the importance of ritual. When grief ministers have a good appreciation of what rituals accomplish, they find themselves far more effective in communicating with the bereaved. Rituals have a very valuable and healing role with those who are suffering a loss. Through rituals we are aided in adjusting to loss. Ritual gestures and actions along with symbols greatly influence the grieving process. When the bereaved participate in rituals, they are becoming aware of the need to express their innermost emotions utilizing words and gestures as vehicles.

We noted in the chapter on journal writing that according to Henri Nouwen we need to visit the place of our own powerlessness. The experience of loss in death makes us feel helpless. We are off balance and our physical, emotional, and spiritual life yearns for stability. Through rituals we act out in healthy and healing ways how we really feel during a critical time in our lives. Rituals connect us with our own scattered and often fragmented feelings. At the same time they assist us in accepting the reality of our losses. They help us to overcome practicing avoidance and denial of losses by being present and engaging the ritual draws us into the faith embrace where losses are put into the larger perspective.

Pastoral Scenario

The following pastoral scenario illustrates the possible setting for meeting with families in order to prepare the funeral liturgy.

Mary as a parish grief minister made an appointment to meet with the Jones family. It is 1:00 p.m. and the appointment will take place in the parish center office. There are a number of ministers in the parish Ministry of Consolation. Mary's role is to assist the bereaved in preparing the funeral Mass. She is familiar with all of the moments or stations as they are put forth in the *Order of Christian Funerals*. The family is primarily concerned about what they can do during the Mass.

When Mary entered the parish office, she saw two familiar faces. There were four people waiting for her. It was the family of Mr. Jones who had been one of Mary's Communion visitations. Mary had visited Mr. Jones throughout his illness and was with him when hospice workers were there with him at the end of a very lengthy illness. It was fortunate that she already knew the family. After some brief introductions and words of condolence to the other relatives, she made some remarks as to how important the liturgy is for everyone. The family responded expressing their wishes. Mary was very aware of the circumstances of the death and this helped her in making preparations.

Mary easily explained that according to our Catholic ritual there are many options and ways for families to participate and minister. The family responded with interest and questions about how to approach the actual funeral.

Mary, as a grief minister, gave a very fine presentation which served as an overview to the ritual. She communicated to the bereaved that when we think of the funeral as the completion of the journey begun in baptism then everything is much easier to appreciate and understand. The liturgy itself teaches and instills a deep realization that the death of a Christian is a sacred time for all.

Mary explained that the symbols associated with baptism illustrate during the liturgy how the gathering together of the family and friends completes the deceased's earthly journey. The use of the white pall on the casket along with holy water symbolizes the white garment and holy water during baptism. The Easter candle gives hope in the resurrection. As we died to sin and rose in hope in baptism, now we recall this as the earthly journey ends. The signs, symbols, and rituals that were interwoven throughout our faith life now come together to complete the tapestry of a Christian life. Sacred signs, symbols, and images send significant messages of faith to the assembly. They help us to experience the spiritual transformations so necessary for spiritual acceptance of loss.

Mary gave the family a very consoling thought as a grief minister about the liturgy. She told them that so many years ago when the deceased was an infant he was carried into the assembly of faith by relatives and friends. Now, in death his body is once again carried into the assembly by this generation of family and friends to pray for him that he will go forth to the Kingdom of Heaven.

Such images give added emphasis and consolation to those asked to participate in the ritual. Those invited to the ministry of pall bearers to carry the deceased Christian into the Church should be reminded of the importance of this role. The family in the gathering area places the while pall over the casket. A hymn of hope is sung as the procession takes place. Even though there are tears in our eyes, they do not obscure the symbols of hope and a vision of eternal life for our loved one when we will once again be with them.

Liturgical Consolation

As the grief minister, Mary communicates to the family the rich resource of faith evident in the Catholic funeral ritual. The consoling images given in the sacred readings from both the Hebrew Scriptures and the New Testament readings are highlighted in preparing liturgy. Parish ministers either use the actual ritual the *Order of Christian Funerals* or a parish booklet prepared with readings for families to choose for the liturgy.

It is consoling for families to request that a family member or a friend of the family proclaim the readings during the funeral Mass. Before this happens the consoling minister who is pre-

paring with them needs to give some brief instruction about the
lector's ministry. Such a catechesis or instruction will greatly assist a lector especially if they are from another parish.

It is important for Mary in talking with the family about selecting a lector that she keep in mind that being a lector entails
more than just reading in church. A lector is a minister to the assembly and is there to minister to the community. In the instance
of a funeral Mass there are basic needs facing the assembly. The
lector is serving the assembly of faith when he or she proclaims
the scriptures in a consoling way. This means that there has to be
an awareness of the consoling and hopeful themes put forth in
the scriptures surrounding the death of a Christian. Selecting
a lector recommended by the family has to prompt a certain
question. "Has the person been a lector before in church?" "Will
they be able to handle this duty?"

There are other options available for participation by the
family. The presentation of gifts at the Offertory may be done
by family members. It is during the presentation of gifts that we
have seen grandchildren and other young relatives participate
in traditional and unique ways. Young children may be allowed
to bring up a drawing or other small memento for placement at
the foot of the altar.

When meeting with families the grief minister has to approach the "Farewell Remembrance" during the final commen-
dation and farewell in the funeral carefully. There are developing
opinions as to what is the best time to remember the deceased
Christian. Some parishes and dioceses have decided that a
more appropriate time is during the vigil. The grief minister
with the parish staff has to be clear about what policy will be
held by their parish or diocese. Since the promulgation of the
new ritual in 1989, the "remembrance" along with what is appropriate music have been issues which need to be addressed.
In my opinion both of these issues relate to how people appreciate or do not appreciate the sacred nature of liturgy. While it is
very understandable that emotions while grieving are very intense, there does have to be an order and sacred way of celebrating funeral Masses. Usually there are not difficulties with those
who are members of the worshiping community. I have found

most of the problems arise in our secular society with those who are "unchurched" and are not familiar with the need for guidelines from dioceses and parishes.

One of the more difficult concerns facing grief ministers is the "Farewell." In many ways it has become part of the culture which holds to the importance of a eulogy. For the secular society a eulogy usually consists of fond memories, some humorous story about what a great person the deceased was. A "remembrance" in the context of the Catholic ritual is a recollection of the deceased life in the spirit. It is always done in the faith context and really seeks to focus on the faith legacy the deceased has left for us. If a person had been dedicated to helping the poor at a soup kitchen, then the remembrance might focus on how the deceased lived out the beatitudes through his or her service and how this dedication challenges us to do the same.

Eulogies are not part of the Catholic tradition. We believe that we are saved not by our own merits but only through Christ. Consequently we remember the deceased Christian in the context of faith. We praise God for the gifts given to the Christian during their earthly life. This emphasis is an expression of trust in God in whom we live and breathe and have our being. All praise must be given to the One who gives life and inspires all that we say and do.

Being with the bereaved is a moment of evangelization. Those who have been away from practicing their faith for years now have an opportunity to find consolation. The consoling minister is the evangelizer. The grief minister can present themes of hope which will cooperate with the working of the Holy Spirit touching the bereaved person's life while they mourn.

Concluding Points

Our consoling minister is with the bereaved and helping them to find meaning in the way the funeral is celebrated. The minister is faced with those who are still very early in their grief. Being familiar with the early symptoms of grief (see introduction and chapter one) assists the minister with more awareness of what the bereaved are feeling.

A *Liturgy Preparation Sheet* is a valuable tool for the grief minister who is meeting with the bereaved. This pastoral tool can be developed according to individual parish and diocesan needs. It may be adapted to special circumstances that occur.

Please consult the Liturgy Preparation Sheet on page 82.

Sample Liturgy Preparation Sheet

Saint Thomas Aquinas Parish
Nahant, Massachusetts

ORDER OF CHRISTIAN FUNERALS

Liturgy of the Vigil

Time: _____

Place: _____

First Reading _____
Reader: _____
Second Reading _____
Reader: _____

Remembrance _____

Music: _____
(see hymn list)
Other: (photo displays, awards, etc.)
_____
_____
_____
_____
_____
_____

Bereavement Minister:
_____

Life is changed ... not ended

Saint Thomas Aquinas Parish
Nahant, Massachusetts

Funeral Mass

Pall bearers

_____
_____
_____
_____

Pall _____

First Reading
_____

Reader
_____

Second Reading
_____

Reader
_____

Prayer of Faithful Reader
_____

Special remembrance of other relatives
_____

Presentation of gifts:
_____

Special Remembrances / Remembrance:
_____
_____

Music selections (see list):
_____
_____

Grief Minister
as Compassionate Listener

This final chapter is devoted to the consoling minister's role as a compassionate listener. Throughout this book we have explored how we are present to the bereaved in a variety of ministerial roles. In this chapter we will explore how we can effectively be present to the bereaved through being a compassionate listener. This role is woven through all of the many ways we have experienced the Ministry of Consolation.

A basic theme for consoling ministry is that of being a person dedicated to being present to the bereaved. This presence is always active, never passive. In the many ways in which ministry occurs it is essential that we be there for the bereaved when needed. Actively listening allows those who are grieving to find in the grief minister one who is compassionate and caring about how they feel during the shattering experience of intense grief. Active listening means the minister not only hears what is being said, but the minister listens for both nuances and what may be missing. As an active listener we often reflect back to the speaker what they have said while gently nudging them into a more spiritual approach. Consider the following dialogue between our minister, Mary, and a bereaved widow.

Widow: "I need to clean the house now that the funeral is over."
Mary: "What do you think, Bill (the deceased) would want you to do with his clothing?" "Do you have a favorite charity you would like to donate to?"

Stress-Filled Time

Experiencing a significant loss is a chaotic time. Very often the bereaved feel disoriented and confused. This is especially evident with sudden loss and unexpected losses. Disasters, accidents, terrorism, and other events shock us beyond belief. To accept the loss means that we need some way of being able to live with it. We need to communicate our emotions of this experience. We need to tell this story over and over again in order to accept first that it really happened and in so doing also learn to cope with what we are beginning to accept.

On Deaf Ears

It is not uncommon in today's society for people to find ways to not go through grief. Our society as it becomes increasingly secular, does not want to face spiritual eventualities.

Society and our network of friends and acquaintances do not always want to face loss. Usually people are supportive but in very limited ways. During the funeral and for a brief time afterwards they are willing to talk about the loss. Once the bereaved begin to repeat and retell their story, the support disappears. The sad reality about our culture is that there is considerable avoidance of topics and conversations about death.

A Compassionate Listener

There are many prerequisites facing the consoling minister in accepting this way to minister. There has to be a deep commitment to be willing to spend time with the bereaved person. When the minister schedules an appointment to visit, he or she has to be willing to listen without hurrying the bereaved. Sufficient time has to be given for the bereaved to tell their story.

The compassionate listener very often acts as a spiritual as well as an emotional guide for the bereaved. The grief minister has to be familiar with what it means to opt for empathy over sympathy. Our society is very conditioned to being sympathetic. This is evident at the time of a funeral. During the wake a very awkward time for many is when they express "sympathy." Sympathy is a passing and very objective expression. We hear people say the words "I am sorry for your loss," or they may say "Please accept our condolences." Both of these remarks while well-intentioned do not really engage the bereaved.

Consoling ministers who want to be with the bereaved have to be empathic. Empathy is when we see ourselves in another's position. The empathic statement is "It must be very difficult for you." This is by far more engaging. It gives the bereaved permission to make an active response. They may tell us: "I am feeling as if part of me has died." Or "This is so painful yet I am beginning to accept this."

Listening is a key for all of the ministry times we have explored in this book. It is the essential backdrop for ministry. Listening means empowering the bereaved to feel that their cries have been heard. So many times they feel that everything is falling on deaf ears.

Sharpening Our Listening Skills

It is necessary to have an active presence with the bereaved. We cannot be passive or detached if we want to be an effective listener. The consoling grief minister has to be willing to explore better ways to hear what the bereaved person is communicating. Developing and sharpening up on listening skills is essential.

The good listener does not just silently observe or act as some sort of a container or receptacle to what is being voiced. This passive receiving of thoughts and emotions could do considerable harm. It may drive the bereaved into the doldrums of confusion and make them feel more isolated. The active listener is one who is able to provide some verbal feedback to the bereaved. This may be accomplished with short statements or summaries of what has been communicated. These verbal and non-verbal cues demonstrate to the speaker that you are listening.

It takes time and formation to give the bereaved verbal feedback. Many parishes and institutions practice role playing just to acquaint the minister with ways to improve as an active listener. The ability to give feedback relies on the minister's ability to create a mental image or model in their mind of what is being said.

This allows for them to be empathic to feel with the bereaved and, through an awareness of the grieving process and its components, filter what is being felt and communicated by the bereaved.

Healing Ways to Hear

The following steps help in becoming an effective listener. These steps help us keep in mind what is necessary to truly communicate with those who need to tell their story.

1. **Develop a presence.** Physically face the one who is speaking to you.

2. **Be attentive.** Stay focused yet relax as you listen.

3. **Create a mental picture.** Try to visualize what is being told to you.

4. **Do not try to fix things.** Allow the story to be told as it is.

5. **Do not try to rescue people.** Don't give your solution to problems.

6. **Allow for silences.** Pauses are meant for people to collect thoughts. Wait for them to gather thoughts.

7. **Try to be empathic.** Try to feel what they are feeling in their story.

8. **Give feedback.** Summarize, acknowledge feelings.

9. **Be aware of bodily expression.** Posture, gestures, and other non-verbal indicators of emotions.

10. **Allow time.** Do not rush the bereaved. Set aside time for them.

Condolence Call

There are people in our society who become invisible. They are invisible as people choose not to hear or see what they are really all about. We find this very often with the mentally challenged, the physically challenged, those suffering from terminal illness such as AIDS, victims of domestic violence, and those who are suffering from grief. Our concern is with how we can improve our ability to see and listen to the bereaved in more compassionate ways. We need to as consoling ministers instruct our parish communities about the needs facing those who are facing loss in their lives. The following phone conversation illustrates the need to fine tune our listening skills when communicating with the bereaved. Are they in need of ministry? Do they need a condolence call from the grief minister?

Pastoral Scenario

Marian was just recently widowed. She is seventy-two years old and enjoyed forty-three years of marriage. She had the following conversation on the phone with a parish grief minister (G.M.)

> Marian: "Hello, I would like to arrange a "month's mind" Mass for my late husband Charles S."

> G.M.: "Oh, yes, Mrs. S. I recall talking with you at the funeral. I hope you are better."

> Marian: (pause) "It's getting worse rather than better."

> G.M.: "I am sorry to hear that. It is still so very early and it must be difficult for you."

> Marian: "I feel so alone and sometimes I think he'll come in the door any minute."

> G.M.: "We have some fine people who visit people who have had recent losses. Would you like to hear from someone soon."

> Marian: "Oh, thank you. I would like to receive a visit. It is so lonely and quiet here."

Listening Points

When we are with the bereaved we have to be aware of what to listen for in their conversations. Listening points are times that strike us as a need facing the bereaved. In this previous pastoral scenario, there are a variety of points. We note them from the beginning when Marian mentions how things are getting worse a point is made. Marian is now moving away from being numbed by the loss and into a phase where reality is setting in for her. The more the brief conversations continues we hear her cry as an isolated person. She now finds herself alone after the funeral. She is asking for consolation by calling about the memorial Mass. Marian's acceptance of having someone visit her is another point in the conversation which must be heard.

The more familiar we are with the needs facing the bereaved the better we can minister. The grief minister brings consolation by listening as a person trained to hear in light of an awareness as to what people are going through while they grieve.

Developing Listening Skills

Becoming a good compassionate listener is an ongoing process. We have to be aware of techniques which are useful not only with the bereaved but with others as well. If we are a good listener in our lives, it will translate into a skill which we know is valuable for the grief-stricken. Some of the following points will make us more effective. Remember we need to practice these techniques.

1. **Stay focused.** We need to be attentive and not suffer distractions such as watching television or listening to the radio or glancing at a magazine.

2. **Allow the person to speak.** The whole idea of listening is defeated when we interrupt a person. Bodily gestures such as placing our hands over our mouth or our chin in our hands can remind us to be quiet.

3. **Avoid being judgmental.** Being defensive and looking for what is right or wrong will not enhance listening.

4. **Avoid non-verbal signals.** There are non-verbal indicators you may make such as shrugging your shoulders, using a different tone of voice, looking away from someone, loss of eye contact, rolling your eyes or other gestures which are statements in themselves even when they are partially expressed.

5. **Avoid advice.** Eventually you may be asked to give advice. Do not offer it initially unless asked to do so.

You may and probably will come up with some more ideas about techniques and listening skills. Allowing others to speak and feel heard is the compassionate way to listen.

Conclusion

This chapter is a fitting conclusion for this book. It highlights the importance of the consoling ministry to give voice to those who are trying to express themselves while they grieve. In retrospect it should be evident that this chapter has been an underlying theme for the multifaceted ministry of consoling. The consoling minister who is an empathic listener is the one who can be a healing instrument for so many. Our hopeful prayer is that all of us will progress in better ways to constantly improve the gifts given to us to help those who are grieving as consoling ministers.

Notes

[1] *Order of Christian Funerals,* General Introduction, par. 8.

[2] Terence Curley. *Console One Another: A Guide For Christian Funerals.* Sheed and Ward, Mich., 1993 (cf. 72).

[3] *Console One Another.* Ibid. (ch. 2 The Ritual's Symbols for Support) 13.

[4] Terence P. Curley. *Healing the Broken-Hearted: Consoling the Grief-Stricken.* Alba House, New York, 1995 (cf. ch. 3 "Initiating A Parish Bereavement Committee").

[5] Gerald G. May, M.D. *Care of Mind, Care of Spirit: A Psychiatrist Explores Spiritual Direction.* Harper San Francisco, 1982, 8.

[6] "People Don't Just Die: The Role of Hospice" by Stephanie Thibeault. http://www.grieflossrecovery.com.

[7] Ibid., Thibeault, 1.

[8] Carolyn Gratton. *The Art of Spiritual Guidance.* Crossroad Publishing Co., New York, 1992, 138–39.

[9] Terence Curley. *Console One Another: A Guide for Christian Funerals.* Sheed & Ward, Wis., 1993, (See schemata of funeral journey, Appendix C, 91.)

[10] Henri Nouwen. *The Inner Voice of Love: A Journey Through Anguish to Freedom.* Doubleday, New York, 1996, 30.

[11] Terence Curley. *Six Steps for Managing Loss: A Catholic Guide Through Grief.* Alba House, New York, 1997, 4–11 (Steps adapted to Grief).

[12] Terence P. Curley. *The Ministry of Consolation: A Parish Guide for Comforting the Bereaved.* Alba House, New York, 1993. (See ch. 3 "Grief Through the Eyes of a Child.")

[13] Claudia L. Jewett. *Helping Children Cope with Separation and Loss.* The Harvard Common Press, Boston, Mass. 1982, 8–9.

[14] Terence P. Curley. Ibid. 14–15 (Prayer Service Outline for Children).

[15] Terence P. Curley. *Console One Another: A Guide for Christian Funerals.* Sheed & Ward, Kansas City, Mo., 1993.

[16] Michael R. Leming and George E. Dickinson. *Understanding Dying, Death, and Bereavement.* Holt, Rinehart, and Winston, New York, 1985, 132 (quote by Helen Galen).

[17] Barbara F. Meltz. "Helping Children Live Through Loss and Grief," *The Boston Globe.* September, 1993, A–4 (quote by: Rabbi Earl Grollman).

[18] Mary DeTurris Poust. *Parenting A Grieving Child.* Loyola Press, Chicago, 2002. (Cf. ch. 9, "Ways To Remember: Ritual and the Creation of Memories" contains interview remarks by Terence P. Curley.)

[19] Terence Curley. *Healing the Broken-Hearted, Consoling the Grief-Stricken.* Alba House, New York, 1995, 62–63 (Anniversary Prayer Service).

[20] Bob Deits. *Life After Loss: A Personal Guide Dealing with Death, Divorce, Job Change, and Relocation.* Fisher Books, Tucson, 1988, 146–47.

[21] Ibid., 149.

[22] Terence Curley. *Six Steps for Managing Loss: A Catholic Guide Through Grief.* Alba House, New York, 1997. (A series of Prayer Experiences are offered, 35–48, which identify Psalm meditations with grief symptoms.)

[23] Henri J.M. Nouwen. *A Letter of Consolation.* Harper San Francisco, 1982.

[24] Ibid., 6.

[25] Ibid., 9.

[26] Curley. *Six Steps for Managing Loss.* Insights are provided through steps for the journey through grief. These steps outline emotions/spirituality connected with the experience of loss.

[27] Terence Curley. "The Teenager's Experience of Loss," *Pastoral Life.* Vol. 46, no. 9, October 1997, 25–31.

[28] Terence Curley. "Healing Grief with a Compassionate Listener," *Pastoral Life.* Vol. 46, no. 4, April, 1997, 13–18.

[29] Paul E. Irion. "The Funeral and the Bereaved," in *Resources for Ministry in Death and Dying.* Eds. Larry A. Platt and Roger C. Branch, Broadman Press, Nashville, 1989, 211.

Grief Topics and Bibliography

References for Consoling Ministry

Clinebell, Howard. *Basic Types of Pastoral Care Counseling, Resources for the Ministry of Healing and Growth.* Abingdon Press, Nashville, 1966, 1984.

Curley, Terence P. *The Ministry of Consolation: A Parish Guide for Comforting the Bereaved.* Alba House, New York, 1993.

———. *Healing the Broken-Hearted, Consoling the Grief-Stricken.* Alba House, New York, 1995.

———. *Six Steps for Managing Loss: A Catholic Guide Through Grief.* Alba House, New York, 1997.

———. "A Bill of Rights for the Bereaved," *Pastoral Life,* vol. 49, no. 1, January, 2000.

Deits, Bob. *Life after Loss: A Personal Guide Dealing with Death, Divorce, Job Change and Re-location.* Fisher Books, Tucson, 1988.

Gerkin, Charles V. *Crisis Experience in Modern Life: Theory and Theology of Pastoral Care.* Abingdon Press, Nashville, 1979.

Gilbert, Richard B. *HeartPeace: Healing Help for Grieving Folks.* Abbey Press, Ind., 1996.

Gilmour, Peter, ed. *Now and at the Hour of Our Death.* Liturgy Training Publications, Chicago, 1989.

Manning, Doug. *Don't Take Away My Grief: What To Do When You Lose a Loved One.* Harper-Collins Publishers, New York, 1979 and 1984.

Michell, Kenneth R., and Herbert Anderson. *All Our Losses, All Our Griefs: Resources for Pastoral Care.* The Westminster Press, Philadelphia, 1983.

Reilly, Donna, and JoAnn Sturzl. *Grief Ministry, Helping Others Mourn.* Resource Publications, San Jose, Calif., 1992.

Liturgy Preparation

Boadt, Lawrence, Mary Dombeck, and H. Richard Rutherford. The Rites of Death and Dying, 1987, National Meeting of the Federation of Diocesan Liturgical Committees. Collegeville, The Liturgical Press, 1988.

Catholic Conference of Canadian Bishops. "The Christian Funeral," National Bulletin on Liturgy, 22, no. 119 (197–257) December, 1989.

Curley, Terence P. *Console One Another: A Guide to Christian Funerals,* Sheed & Ward, Mich. 1993.

———. "Cremation and Bodily Resurrection," *The Priest,* vol. 55, no. 4, April, 1999.

———. "The Order Of Christian Funerals, A Better Connection for Pastoral Care," *The Priest,* vol. 47, no. 4, April, 1991.

———. "The Tenth Anniversary of the Funeral Ritual," *Pastoral Life,* vol. 49, no. 4, April, 2000.

———. "Bringing Order to Funerals," *The Priest,* vol. 56, no. 3, March, 2000.

———. *Healing: Questions and Answers For Those Who Mourn.* Alba House, New York, 2002.

International Commission on English in Liturgy (ICEL). *Order of Christian Funerals.* Washington, D.C., 1989.

———. *Order of Christian Funerals, Appendix 2: Cremation.* Catholic Book Publishing Co., New Jersey, 1997.

Rutherford, H. Richard. *The Death of a Christian.* Collegeville: The Liturgical Press, 1990.

Spakes, Robert, and Richard Rutherford. "The Order of Christian Funerals: A Study in Bereavement and Lament," *Worship,* 60, no. 6, 1986 (499).

Formation and Instruction

Arbuckle, Gerald A. *Change, Grief, and Renewal in the Church: A Spirituality for a New Era.* Christian Classics, Inc. Westminster, Md., 1991.

Curley, Terence P. "The Catechism of the Catholic Church: A Resource for Pastoral Life," *The Priest,* vol. 49, no. 6., June, 1993.

———. "The New Catechism and the RCIA Journey," *Pastoral Life,* vol. 44, no. 2, February, 1994.

———. "'Veritatis Splendor' As Spiritual Direction," *Pastoral Life,* vol. 43, no. 8, September, 1994.

———. "Evangelium Vitae and Our Culture," *The Priest,* vol. 51, no. 10, October, 1995.

———. "The Pursuit of Truth," Viewpoint, *The Priest*, vol. 55, no. 7, July, 1999.

———. "The Office for the Dead: A Parish Prayer," *The Priest,* vol. 52, no. 11, November, 1996.

———. "Spiritual Steps for Managing Loss," *Pastoral Life,* vol. 47, no. 11, 1998.

Gratton, Carolyn. *The Art of Spiritual Direction.* Crossroad, New York, 1998.

Nouwen, Henri J.M. *The Inner Voice of Love.* Doubleday, New York, 1996.

———. "A Letter of Consolation." Harper San Francisco, 1982.

U.S. Catholic Conference. *Catechism of the Catholic Church.* Doubleday, New York, 1984.

———. "Our Hearts Were Burning Within Us," Committee on Education U.S. Catholic Conference, Washington, D.C., 1999.

Lawler, Ronald, Donald W. Wuerl, Thomas C. Lawler. *The Teaching of Christ: A Catholic Catechism for Adults.* Our Sunday Visitor, Indiana, 1979.

McBride, Alfred. *Father McBride's Family Catechism.* Our Sunday Visitor, Indiana, 1987.

The Psalms and Religious Expression

Anderson, Bernhard W. *Out of the Depths: The Psalms Speak for Us Today.* The Westminster Press, Philadelphia, 1983.

Brueggeman, Walter. *The Message of the Psalms: A Theological Commentary.* Augsburg Publishing Co., Minneapolis, 1984.

Craghan, John F. *Psalms for all Seasons.* Collegeville: The Liturgical Press, 1993.

Creach, Jerome F. D. *Psalms.* Interpretation Bible Studies. Geneva Press, Kentucky, 1998.

Dollen, Charles. *Prayer Book of the King: The Psalms.* Alba House, New York, 1998.

Quillo, Ronald. *The Psalms: Prayers of Many Moods.* Paulist Press, New Jersey, 1998.

Grief Support

Curley, Terence. *A Way of the Cross for the Bereaved.* Alba House, New York, 1996.

Elordi, Barbara, Jessie Flynn, Marlene Duffy. *Ministry of Consolation Training Manual.* National Catholic Ministry to the Bereaved. For further information contact the Office of the National Catholic Ministry to the Bereaved, 28700 Euclid Ave., Cleveland, OH (440) 943–3480.

Gilbert, Richard B. *Finding Your Way After Your Parent Dies.* Ave Maria Press, Notre Dame, Ind., 1999.

O'Brien, Maureen. *Praying Through Grief, Healing Prayer Services for Those Who Mourn.* Ave Maria Press, Ind., 1997.

———. *The New Day Journal: A Journey from Grief to Healing,* ACTA Publications, Chicago, 2000.

Internet

www.StThomasNahant.com

Audio Visual Guides for Good Grief

The following audio-visuals are by Fr. Terence Curley:

From Darkness to Light: A Healing Path Through Grief. Alba House Communications, Canfield, Ohio. This is a four-part audio which provides the listener with healing ways to go through grief. The tape provides an overview of the grieving process, explanation of symptoms, and helpful ways to place the loss into the context of faith. (Available through Andrew Lane Co., 800-451-2520.)

Through the Dark Valley: Healing Steps for Managing Loss. Alba House Communications, Canfield, Ohio. This four-part video presentation further explains Father Curley's title *Six Steps for Managing Loss.* The presentation gives effective steps for managing our losses. It develops a spirituality for those who are grieving. (Available through Andrew Lane Co., 800-451-2520.)

Journey to Healing: A Ministry for the Bereaved. Alba House Communications, Canfield, Ohio. This four-part video is used as an introduction for grief ministers, support groups, bereavement committees, and those who are grieving. It is insightful about the dynamics and taking the journey through grief. (Available through Andrew Lane Co., 800-451-2520.)

Arise and Walk: A Christian Grieving Guide. Alba House Communications, Canfield, Ohio. This four-part video explores spirituality for the bereaved. It outlines ways to express loss in the context of faith. The video is formatted for retreats, days of recollection and other pastoral presentations. (Available through Andrew Lane Co., 800-451-2520.)

Other Titles by Terence P. Curley

Console One Another: A Guide for Christian Funerals, Sheed & Ward, Michigan, 1993.

The Ministry of Consolation: A Parish Guide for Comforting the Bereaved, Alba House, New York, 1993.

Healing the Broken-Hearted: Consoling the Grief-Stricken, Alba House, New York, 1995.

A Way of the Cross for the Bereaved, Alba House, New York, 1995.

Six Steps for Managing Loss: A Catholic Guide Through Grief, Alba House, New York, 1997.

Healing: Questions and Answers for Those Who Mourn, Alba House, New York, 2002.

Journey To Healing: A Ministry for the Bereaved (video), Alba House Communications, Canfield, Ohio, 1996.

Through the Dark Valley (video), Alba House Communications, Canfield Ohio, 1998.

From Darkness to Light (audio), Alba House Communications, Canfield, Ohio, 1998.

Arise & Walk: A Christian Grieving Guide (video), Alba House Communications, Canfield, Ohio, 2001.